MASTERING RUST

SAFE AND EFFICIENT PROGRAMMING

FIRST EDITION

Preface

Rust is a programming language that has revolutionized systems programming by offering unparalleled performance and memory safety. As the demands for secure, efficient, and reliable software grow, Rust has emerged as a powerful tool for developers worldwide. This book, designed as an all-encompassing guide, will take you through the journey of learning Rust, from its foundational concepts to its advanced features and real-world applications.

Each chapter in this book has been carefully crafted to build upon the previous, ensuring a seamless learning experience. The introductory chapters provide a solid understanding of what Rust is and why it matters in the modern programming landscape. As you progress, you'll explore Rust's core concepts, from ownership and borrowing to its unique approach to memory safety.

For those who are new to Rust, the early chapters will guide you through installation, writing your first program, and understanding the toolchain. Intermediate chapters delve into the language's building blocks, the borrow checker, and advanced features like traits, generics, and concurrency. You will also gain insight into Rust's vibrant ecosystem, tools, and package management system.

The book doesn't stop at theory. It explores Rust's practical applications, from systems programming to web development and game design. For those looking to optimize their Rust programs, a dedicated chapter focuses on performance tuning, memory management, and idiomatic Rust practices.

As you near the end, you will find discussions on Rust's interoperability with other languages, its future trends, and how you can contribute to the Rust community. Finally, the appendices serve as a handy reference for terms, resources, sample projects, and FAQs, ensuring you have all the support you need to master Rust.

Whether you are a beginner or an experienced developer looking to add Rust to your skillset, this book aims to equip you with the knowledge and confidence to harness Rust's full potential. Welcome to your Rust journey!

Table of Contents

Chapter 1: Introduction to Rust

What is Rust?

Rust is a modern systems programming language designed with the dual goals of safety and performance. Released by Mozilla Research in 2010, Rust has grown in popularity for its ability to deliver low-level control akin to C and C++, while significantly reducing the risks associated with memory errors, data races, and undefined behavior.

At its core, Rust addresses some of the most critical challenges in software development:

1. **Memory Safety**: Rust eliminates common memory issues like null pointer dereferencing, buffer overflows, and use-after-free errors. It achieves this without the need for a garbage collector.
2. **Concurrency**: Rust provides robust concurrency mechanisms that ensure thread safety, preventing data races at compile time.
3. **Performance**: Rust offers performance comparable to C and C++, making it suitable for high-performance applications like operating systems, game engines, and web servers.
4. **Expressiveness**: Rust's rich type system, pattern matching, and expressive syntax allow developers to write clean and maintainable code.

A Brief History of Rust

Rust was initially conceived by Graydon Hoare at Mozilla Research as a personal project before gaining institutional backing. Its development was driven by the need for a language that could address the shortcomings of existing systems programming languages, particularly in areas like memory safety and concurrency. Over the years, Rust has undergone significant evolution, culminating in its first stable release, version 1.0, in May 2015.

Since then, Rust has seen widespread adoption across industries. Major tech companies like Microsoft, Amazon, and Google have integrated Rust into their development pipelines, citing its reliability and performance.

Key Features of Rust

Ownership Model

One of Rust's defining features is its ownership model. Unlike other languages that rely on garbage collection or manual memory management, Rust enforces strict ownership rules at compile time. Every value in Rust has a single owner, and when the owner goes out of scope, the value is automatically deallocated. This ensures memory safety and eliminates common bugs without runtime overhead.

Borrowing and References

Rust introduces the concepts of borrowing and references to manage data access. Borrowing allows multiple parts of a program to access a value without transferring ownership. Rust distinguishes between mutable and immutable references, ensuring that data can only be mutated through a single reference at a time.

Type System

Rust's powerful type system includes features like enums, structs, and traits. Enums in Rust are more expressive than those in many other languages, allowing you to define data structures with associated values. Traits enable polymorphism and code reuse, making it easy to write generic and extensible code.

Fearless Concurrency

Concurrency is a cornerstone of modern programming, and Rust excels in this domain. By leveraging the ownership and type system, Rust ensures that concurrent code is free of data races. Developers can write multi-threaded programs with confidence, knowing that the compiler enforces safety guarantees.

Cargo and Crates

Rust comes with Cargo, its built-in package manager and build system. Cargo simplifies dependency management, project compilation, and testing. The Rust ecosystem is rich with libraries, or "crates," available on Crates.io, the central repository for Rust packages.

Why Rust Matters

Rust has become a language of choice for developers tackling complex systems programming tasks. Its adoption spans domains such as:

- **Operating Systems**: Rust is used in projects like Redox OS and components of the Linux kernel.
- **Web Development**: Frameworks like Actix and Rocket make Rust a strong contender for building web applications.
- **Game Development**: Rust's performance and safety features are well-suited for game engines and real-time applications.
- **Embedded Systems**: Rust's low-level control and safety make it ideal for resource-constrained environments.

A Simple Rust Example

To illustrate Rust's simplicity and safety, consider the following program that calculates the factorial of a number:

```
fn factorial(n: u32) -> u32 {
    match n {
        0 | 1 => 1,
```

```
        _ => n * factorial(n - 1),
    }
}

fn main() {
    let number = 5;
    println!("The factorial of {} is {}", number, factorial(number));
}
```

In this program:

1. The `factorial` function uses pattern matching to handle base cases and recursion.
2. Rust's strong type system ensures that the input and output types are consistent.
3. Memory safety is guaranteed without the need for explicit deallocation.

Conclusion

Rust is more than just a programming language; it is a paradigm shift in how developers approach systems programming. By combining safety, performance, and expressiveness, Rust empowers developers to build robust, high-performance applications with confidence. This chapter serves as a gateway to understanding why Rust has become a cornerstone of modern software development. In the next chapters, we will dive deeper into Rust's features and capabilities, beginning with setting up your development environment.

The Rise of Systems Programming

Systems programming has been at the forefront of computing since the advent of modern computer systems. It represents the foundation upon which software interacts directly with hardware, orchestrating processes that underpin operating systems, compilers, network stacks, and embedded systems. With the growing complexity and scale of modern applications, the need for reliable, efficient, and secure systems programming languages has never been greater. Rust has risen to meet this need, offering solutions to long-standing challenges in systems development.

The Evolution of Systems Programming Languages

Systems programming has traditionally been dominated by low-level languages like Assembly, C, and later C++. Each of these languages brought new capabilities and abstractions that pushed the boundaries of what developers could achieve:

1. **Assembly**: The earliest systems programming relied on Assembly, which provided direct control over hardware but required significant effort to manage complexity and maintain code.

2. **C**: Introduced in the 1970s, C revolutionized systems programming by providing a higher-level abstraction while retaining close-to-hardware control. Its simplicity, portability, and performance led to widespread adoption.
3. **C++**: Building on C, C++ introduced object-oriented programming, further empowering developers to structure their code and manage large-scale systems.

While C and C++ remain staples in systems programming, they are not without flaws. Issues like memory corruption, undefined behavior, and data races have long plagued these languages. The rise of multicore processors and concurrent programming has exacerbated these challenges, making safety-critical applications increasingly difficult to write and maintain.

The Shift Toward Safety and Performance

In recent years, the industry has sought solutions that combine the low-level control of C and C++ with modern safety guarantees. This shift is driven by several key trends:

1. **Security Concerns**: Memory vulnerabilities, such as buffer overflows and null pointer dereferences, account for a significant portion of security exploits. Languages like C and C++ offer little in terms of built-in protections against these issues.
2. **Concurrency**: With the proliferation of multicore processors, concurrent programming has become essential for performance. However, traditional systems programming languages provide limited tools for ensuring safe concurrency.
3. **Complexity of Modern Systems**: The scale and complexity of modern software systems demand better abstractions and tooling to maintain code quality and reduce bugs.

How Rust Addresses These Challenges

Rust was designed from the ground up to address the core issues that have long hindered systems programming. It introduces a novel combination of features that make it a game-changer in this field:

Memory Safety Without Garbage Collection

Rust enforces memory safety through its ownership model. Every value in Rust has a unique owner, and the compiler ensures that there are no dangling pointers, double frees, or other memory-related issues. Unlike garbage-collected languages, Rust's memory safety comes with zero runtime overhead, making it ideal for performance-critical applications.

Consider this example of memory safety in Rust:

```
fn main() {
    let data = String::from("Hello, Rust!");
    let reference = &data; // Borrowing the value

    println!("{}", reference); // Safe to use
    // data is still valid here because the borrow has ended
```

```
}
```

In this example, Rust's borrow checker ensures that `data` remains valid as long as it is being referenced, preventing memory-related bugs at compile time.

Concurrency Made Fearless

Rust's approach to concurrency is another key innovation. By leveraging the ownership model, Rust ensures that data races cannot occur. This is achieved through strict rules about ownership and borrowing that are enforced at compile time.

For instance, the following code illustrates thread-safe concurrency in Rust:

```rust
use std::thread;

fn main() {
    let mut data = vec![1, 2, 3];
    let handle = thread::spawn(move || {
        data.push(4); // Ownership of `data` is moved into the thread
        println!("{:?}", data);
    });

    handle.join().unwrap();
}
```

Here, Rust's ownership system ensures that `data` cannot be accessed simultaneously by multiple threads, preventing potential data races.

Performance Without Compromise

Rust's performance rivals that of C and C++ thanks to its low-level control and lack of garbage collection. Developers can write highly optimized code without sacrificing safety or readability.

For example, consider the use of iterators in Rust, which allow for concise and efficient data processing:

```rust
fn main() {
    let numbers = vec![1, 2, 3, 4, 5];
    let doubled: Vec<_> = numbers.iter().map(|x| x * 2).collect();

    println!("{:?}", doubled); // [2, 4, 6, 8, 10]
}
```

Rust's iterators are designed to avoid unnecessary allocations, ensuring optimal performance.

Adoption Across Industries

Rust's unique blend of safety, performance, and modern features has led to its adoption in a wide range of industries:

- **Operating Systems**: Projects like Redox OS and Rust's integration into the Linux kernel demonstrate its suitability for system-level programming.
- **Web Services**: Companies like Cloudflare and Discord use Rust for high-performance network services and backend development.
- **Embedded Systems**: Rust's low memory footprint and safety guarantees make it ideal for embedded and IoT devices.
- **Game Development**: Game engines like Bevy are leveraging Rust for its performance and reliability.

A Growing Ecosystem and Community

The rise of Rust is also fueled by its thriving ecosystem and supportive community. Tools like Cargo and Rustfmt simplify project management and code formatting, while the extensive library of crates on Crates.io accelerates development.

Moreover, Rust's community actively contributes to its growth through open-source projects, educational resources, and forums like the Rust Users Forum and Rust subreddit.

Conclusion

The rise of systems programming reflects the evolving needs of modern software development. As a language that combines safety, performance, and expressiveness, Rust is redefining what is possible in this domain. By addressing the shortcomings of traditional languages, Rust empowers developers to build the next generation of secure, efficient, and reliable systems. As we delve deeper into Rust's features and capabilities in the chapters ahead, its role in the rise of systems programming will become increasingly evident.

Why Choose Rust?

Choosing a programming language is a critical decision for any developer or team. It affects the efficiency of development, the quality of the final product, and the ability to maintain and scale the codebase over time. Rust, as a modern systems programming language, has carved out a unique position in the programming landscape by addressing the limitations of older languages like C and C++ while introducing innovative features tailored to modern development needs.

Safety Without Sacrificing Performance

Rust's most compelling feature is its ability to ensure memory safety without relying on a garbage collector. This is a significant departure from many modern languages that trade performance for safety. Rust achieves this through its ownership system, a compile-time feature that enforces strict rules on how memory is accessed and modified.

For example, consider the following code snippet demonstrating Rust's ownership rules:

```
fn main() {
    let s1 = String::from("hello");
    let s2 = s1; // Ownership of `s1` is moved to `s2`

    // println!("{}", s1); // This line would cause a compile-time
error
    println!("{}", s2); // `s2` now owns the value
}
```

In this example, Rust ensures that only one owner exists for a piece of data at a time. This eliminates issues like dangling pointers and double frees, which are common in languages without garbage collection.

Comparison with C and C++

In C and C++, developers must manually manage memory, which is both error-prone and time-consuming. A simple mistake, such as forgetting to free allocated memory, can lead to memory leaks or undefined behavior. Rust eliminates this entire class of bugs by making memory safety the responsibility of the compiler.

Furthermore, Rust's memory management model incurs zero runtime cost. Unlike garbage-collected languages such as Java or Go, Rust does not introduce unpredictable pauses for garbage collection, making it suitable for real-time systems and performance-critical applications.

Concurrency Made Simple and Safe

Concurrency is one of the most challenging aspects of modern programming. Traditional systems programming languages provide minimal safeguards against common concurrency issues, such as data races. Rust, on the other hand, makes concurrent programming both simpler and safer through its ownership model and type system.

Consider a simple example of concurrent data manipulation in Rust:

```
use std::sync::Mutex;
use std::thread;
```

```rust
fn main() {
    let data = Mutex::new(0);

    let handles: Vec<_> = (0..10).map(|_| {
        let data = data.clone();
        thread::spawn(move || {
            let mut lock = data.lock().unwrap();
            *lock += 1;
        })
    }).collect();

    for handle in handles {
        handle.join().unwrap();
    }

    println!("Result: {}", *data.lock().unwrap());
}
```

In this code, Rust uses a `Mutex` to safely share data between threads. The compiler ensures that all accesses to the shared data are properly synchronized, preventing data races.

Fearless Concurrency

Rust's fearless concurrency model enables developers to write multi-threaded programs without worrying about subtle bugs that can lead to crashes or corrupted data. By enforcing thread safety at compile time, Rust allows developers to focus on solving problems rather than debugging concurrency issues.

Expressiveness and Flexibility

Rust is not just about safety and performance; it is also a highly expressive language that enables developers to write clean, concise, and maintainable code. Its syntax is designed to be intuitive and ergonomic, allowing developers to quickly adapt to its features.

For example, Rust's pattern matching capabilities provide a powerful way to handle different cases in code:

```rust
fn describe_number(num: i32) -> &'static str {
    match num {
        1 => "One",
        2 => "Two",
        3..=10 => "Between three and ten",
        _ => "Something else",
```

```
        }
    }

fn main() {
    println!("{}", describe_number(5)); // Outputs: Between three and
ten
}
```

Pattern matching in Rust goes beyond simple conditional checks, enabling developers to write expressive code for complex scenarios.

Traits and Generics

Rust's trait system allows for polymorphism and code reuse, making it easy to write generic and reusable components. For example:

```
fn print_items<T: std::fmt::Debug>(items: &[T]) {
    for item in items {
        println!("{:?}", item);
    }
}

fn main() {
    let numbers = vec![1, 2, 3];
    let words = vec!["hello", "world"];

    print_items(&numbers);
    print_items(&words);
}
```

This code demonstrates how Rust's traits and generics enable developers to write functions that work with multiple types while maintaining type safety.

Strong Ecosystem and Tooling

Rust's ecosystem is one of its greatest strengths. The language comes with Cargo, a powerful build system and package manager that simplifies dependency management and project setup. Developers can easily create new projects, add dependencies, and run tests using simple commands:

```
cargo new my_project
```

```
cd my_project
cargo build
cargo run
```

Additionally, Rust's standard library and community-contributed crates provide robust solutions for common programming tasks. The growing ecosystem of libraries and tools ensures that developers can find reliable solutions for their needs without reinventing the wheel.

Integration with Existing Codebases

Rust's ability to interoperate with C and other languages makes it an excellent choice for integrating into existing projects. Using Rust's unsafe keyword, developers can call C functions and work with raw pointers when necessary, ensuring compatibility with legacy systems.

```
extern "C" {
    fn c_function(x: i32) -> i32;
}

fn main() {
    unsafe {
        let result = c_function(42);
        println!("Result from C: {}", result);
    }
}
```

This flexibility allows teams to adopt Rust incrementally, starting with performance-critical or safety-sensitive components.

Community and Support

The Rust community is known for its welcoming and inclusive nature. From the official Rust forums to user groups and online resources, developers have access to a wealth of knowledge and support. The Rust team actively engages with the community to gather feedback and improve the language, ensuring that it evolves to meet the needs of developers.

Long-Term Viability

Rust's backing by major tech companies and its rapid adoption across industries signal its long-term viability. Organizations like Microsoft, Google, and AWS have incorporated Rust into their workflows, further validating its effectiveness and reliability.

Conclusion

Rust stands out as a language that bridges the gap between low-level control and high-level safety. By addressing the challenges of traditional systems programming languages and introducing modern features, Rust has become a compelling choice for developers across domains. Whether you are building performance-critical applications, ensuring safety in concurrent environments, or writing maintainable and expressive code, Rust offers the tools to achieve your goals. Its unique combination of features and the vibrant ecosystem make Rust a language worth choosing for both present and future projects.

Chapter 2: Getting Started with Rust

Installing Rust and Setting Up Your Environment

Rust is a powerful systems programming language that prioritizes safety and performance. Before diving into writing Rust programs, setting up the development environment is a crucial step to ensure a seamless experience. This section covers the installation process, tools, and configurations necessary to get started with Rust development on various operating systems.

Installing Rust

The official Rust team maintains an installer called `rustup`, which is the recommended way to install Rust. `rustup` is a toolchain installer and manager that makes it easy to install and update Rust versions.

Steps to Install Rust

Download   and   Install   `rustup`
Open your terminal or command prompt and run the following command:
bash

```
curl --proto '=https' --tlsv1.2 -sSf https://sh.rustup.rs | sh
```

1. This command downloads and executes the `rustup` installer script. Follow the on-screen instructions to complete the installation. By default, this installs the latest stable version   of   Rust.
    For Windows users, you can download and run the installer from the official Rust website.

Verify   Installation
After installation, restart your terminal and verify that Rust is installed by checking the version:
bash

```
rustc --version
```

2. This command should display the installed version of `rustc` (the Rust compiler).

Configure   Environment   Variables
During installation, `rustup` sets up environment variables for you. If you encounter issues, ensure the `~/.cargo/bin` directory is in your system's PATH.
For   Linux   and   macOS:
bash

```
echo 'export PATH="$HOME/.cargo/bin:$PATH"' >> ~/.bashrc
source ~/.bashrc
```

For Windows, modify your system's PATH variable through the Control Panel or use PowerShell:
powershell

```
[System.Environment]::SetEnvironmentVariable("Path",
"$env:Path;C:\Users\<YourUsername>\.cargo\bin",
[System.EnvironmentVariableTarget]::User)
```

3.

Installing Specific Versions of Rust

If you need a specific version of Rust, use the following command:

```
rustup install <version>
```

For example:

```
rustup install 1.70.0
```

You can switch between installed versions using:

```
rustup default <version>
```

Nightly and Beta Versions

Rust offers nightly and beta channels for developers who want early access to upcoming features:

```
rustup install nightly
rustup default nightly
```

Setting Up a Code Editor

While Rust code can be written in any text editor, using an Integrated Development Environment (IDE) or a code editor with Rust support can enhance productivity. Popular choices include:

Visual Studio Code (VS Code)
Install the Rust Analyzer extension for syntax highlighting, code completion, and other helpful features.

bash

```bash
code --install-extension rust-lang.rust-analyzer
```

1.
2. **JetBrains**   **CLion**
   CLion provides robust support for Rust through the Rust plugin. It integrates with `cargo` and offers debugging tools.
3. **Neovim**   **or**   **Vim**
   For developers who prefer terminal-based editors, plugins like `rust.vim` and `coc-rust-analyzer` provide Rust support.
4. **Other**   **Editors**
   Editors like Sublime Text and Atom also support Rust through community plugins.

Testing the Installation

Create a new Rust project to ensure your setup works correctly.

Create   **a**   **New**   **Project**
Use   the   `cargo`   command   to   create   a   new   project:
bash

```bash
cargo new hello_rust
cd hello_rust
```

This   generates   a   basic   project   structure:
css

```css
hello_rust/
├── Cargo.toml
└── src
    └── main.rs
```

1.

Run   **the**   **Project**
Compile   and   run   the   project   using:
bash

```bash
cargo run
```

This   should   output:

```
Hello, world!
```

2.

Managing Dependencies with `Cargo`

`Cargo` is Rust's package manager and build system. It simplifies dependency management, building, and running projects.

Adding Dependencies

To add a dependency, edit the `Cargo.toml` file in your project's root directory. For example, to add the `rand` crate:

```toml
[dependencies]
rand = "0.8"
```

Run `cargo build` to download and integrate the dependency into your project.

Updating Dependencies

Update all dependencies to their latest compatible versions:

```
cargo update
```

Using Workspaces

Rust allows managing multiple related projects in a single workspace. Create a `Cargo.toml` file in the root directory and define the workspace:

```toml
[workspace]
members = [
    "project_a",
    "project_b",
]
```

Each member directory should contain its own `Cargo.toml` file.

Advanced Configuration

Configuring `rustup`

You can configure `rustup` for specific projects using toolchain overrides:

```
rustup override set nightly
```

To reset to the default toolchain:

```
rustup override unset
```

Using `rustfmt` and `clippy`

Rust provides tools for code formatting and linting:

Install `rustfmt` for consistent code style:
bash

```
rustup component add rustfmt
cargo fmt
```

1.

Install `clippy` for linting:
bash

```
rustup component add clippy
cargo clippy
```

2.

These tools help maintain clean and idiomatic Rust code.

Summary

By following these steps, you have installed Rust, set up a suitable development environment, and tested your setup. With tools like `rustup`, `cargo`, and an appropriate code editor, you're now ready to embark on your Rust programming journey. In the next sections, we'll delve deeper into writing and understanding Rust code.

Writing Your First Rust Program

Writing your first program in Rust is an exciting step that introduces the core structure of a Rust application and the tools you'll use to compile and execute it. In this section, we'll guide you through creating, running, and understanding a basic Rust program while exploring the syntax and features that make Rust unique.

Setting Up the Project

Rust projects are typically managed using `cargo`, the Rust build system and package manager. Start by creating a new project:

Create **a** **New** **Project**
Open your terminal and run:
bash

```
cargo new hello_rust
cd hello_rust
```

This creates a new directory `hello_rust` with the following structure:
css

```
hello_rust/
├── Cargo.toml
└── src
    └── main.rs
```

1.
2. **Open** **the** **Project**
   Navigate into the `hello_rust` directory using your favorite code editor or IDE.

Writing the Program

The default `main.rs` file contains a simple "Hello, world!" program:

```
fn main() {
    println!("Hello, world!");
}
```

This program does the following:

- **Defines a `main` Function**: The `main` function is the entry point of a Rust program.
- **Uses the `println!` Macro**: The `println!` macro prints text to the console.

Modifying the Program

Let's enhance this program to include user input and basic computations. Update `main.rs` with the following code:

```
use std::io;

fn main() {
```

```rust
    println!("Welcome to Rust!");

    println!("Please enter your name:");
    let mut name = String::new();

    io::stdin()
        .read_line(&mut name)
        .expect("Failed to read line");

    println!("Hello, {}! Let's do some math.", name.trim());

    println!("Enter a number:");
    let mut input = String::new();
    io::stdin()
        .read_line(&mut input)
        .expect("Failed to read line");

    let number: i32 = input
        .trim()
        .parse()
        .expect("Please enter a valid number");

    println!("{} squared is {}", number, number * number);
}
```

This program introduces:

- `use std::io`: A standard library module for input/output operations.
- `String`: A growable, UTF-8 encoded string.
- `read_line`: Reads user input from the terminal.
- **Error Handling**: Uses `expect` to handle potential errors gracefully.

Running the Program

Run the program using the following command:

```
cargo run
```

Interact with the program by entering your name and a number. The program will respond dynamically based on your input.

Exploring Rust Syntax and Concepts

Variables and Mutability

Rust variables are immutable by default. Use the `mut` keyword to make them mutable.

```rust
let x = 5; // Immutable variable
let mut y = 10; // Mutable variable
y += 5; // Allowed because y is mutable
```

Data Types

Rust is a statically typed language. Common types include:

- **Primitive Types**: `i32`, `f64`, `bool`, `char`
- **Compound Types**: Tuples and arrays

Example:

```rust
let tuple: (i32, f64, char) = (42, 3.14, 'R');
let array: [i32; 3] = [1, 2, 3];
```

Functions

Rust allows you to define reusable functions:

```rust
fn add(a: i32, b: i32) -> i32 {
    a + b
}

fn main() {
    let result = add(5, 3);
    println!("5 + 3 = {}", result);
}
```

Functions can return values using the last expression or `return` keyword.

Control Flow

Rust supports conditional statements and loops:

```rust
fn main() {
    let number = 7;

    if number % 2 == 0 {
        println!("Even");
    } else {
        println!("Odd");
    }

    for i in 1..=5 {
        println!("Number: {}", i);
    }
}
```

Error Handling

Rust emphasizes robust error handling using `Result` and `Option`.

Unwrapping Results

```rust
use std::fs;

fn main() {
    let contents = fs::read_to_string("example.txt").expect("Failed
to read file");
    println!("File contents: {}", contents);
}
```

Using Match

```rust
fn main() {
    let number: Result<i32, &str> = Ok(10);

    match number {
        Ok(value) => println!("Value: {}", value),
        Err(e) => println!("Error: {}", e),
    }
}
```

Debugging Tips

- Use `println!` to debug values during development.
- Enable Rust's debugging features with tools like `clippy` and `rustfmt`.

Example of debugging output:

```
fn main() {
    let x = 42;
    println!("Debug: x = {}", x);
}
```

Summary

In this section, you wrote and ran your first Rust program, explored core syntax, and learned how to interact with the user and handle errors. This foundational knowledge prepares you for building more complex Rust applications. In the next sections, we'll delve into ownership, borrowing, and the unique features that make Rust stand out.

Understanding the Rust Toolchain

The Rust toolchain is a set of tools and components that work together to enable efficient development in Rust. This section provides a comprehensive overview of the Rust compiler, `cargo`, and additional utilities that streamline the Rust development process. Mastering these tools is essential for writing, building, and managing Rust projects effectively.

Components of the Rust Toolchain

The Rust toolchain consists of the following primary components:

1. `rustc`: **The Rust Compiler**
   The core of the Rust toolchain is `rustc`, the Rust compiler. It translates Rust code into machine code, ensuring safety and performance.
2. `cargo`: **The Rust Build System and Package Manager**
   `cargo` is the centerpiece of the Rust ecosystem, providing functionalities for creating, building, running, and managing Rust projects.
3. **Standard Library (std)**
   Rust comes with a powerful standard library that provides utilities for data structures, I/O operations, threading, and more.
4. `rustup`: **The Rust Toolchain Installer and Manager**
   `rustup` allows developers to install and manage multiple versions of Rust and their associated tools.
5. **Additional Tools**
   Utilities such as `rustfmt` for formatting, `clippy` for linting, and `miri` for interpreting Rust code enhance the developer experience.

The Rust Compiler (`rustc`)

The `rustc` compiler ensures that Rust programs are memory-safe, concurrency-safe, and performant. Most of the time, you interact with `rustc` indirectly through `cargo`, but understanding its basics is helpful.

Basic Usage

You can compile a Rust program directly using `rustc`:

Create a file named `main.rs` with the following content:
rust

```
fn main() {
    println!("Hello, Rust!");
}
```

1.

Compile the program using:
bash

```
rustc main.rs
```

2.

Run the generated executable:
bash

```
./main
```

3.

Compiler Flags

`rustc` supports various flags for debugging, optimization, and output customization. Common flags include:

Debugging Information:
Compile with debugging symbols for use with tools like `gdb`:
bash

```
rustc -g main.rs
```

•

Optimizations:
Use the -O flag for optimized builds:
bash

```
rustc -O main.rs
```

-

Output **Customization**:
Specify the output binary name:
bash

```
rustc -o my_program main.rs
```

-

---

cargo: The Swiss Army Knife of Rust

cargo simplifies Rust project management, from dependency handling to building and testing.

Common Commands
Creating a **Project**
Create a new project using:
bash

```
cargo new my_project
cd my_project
```

1.

Building a **Project**
Build the project:
bash

```
cargo build
```
For optimized builds:
bash

```
cargo build --release
```

2.

Running a **Project**
Run the project:
bash

```
cargo run
```

3.

Testing

Run tests defined in your project:
bash

```
cargo test
```

4.

Cleaning **Up**

Remove build artifacts:
bash

```
cargo clean
```

5.

Checking **Code**

Quickly check for compilation errors without creating an executable:
bash

```
cargo check
```

6.

Dependency Management

cargo uses the Cargo.toml file to manage dependencies. Add a dependency as follows:

```
[dependencies]
serde = "1.0"
```

Update dependencies using:

```
cargo update
```

Workspaces

Workspaces allow managing multiple projects in a single repository. Example Cargo.toml for a workspace:

```
[workspace]
members = [
    "crate_a",
    "crate_b",
]
```

Managing Toolchains with `rustup`

`rustup` enables installing and switching between different Rust versions and channels.

Installing Rust Channels
Stable: The default, production-ready channel.
bash

```
rustup install stable
```

-

Beta: Previews of the next stable release.
bash

```
rustup install beta
```

-

Nightly: Latest features and updates, often experimental.
bash

```
rustup install nightly
```

-

Switch between versions using:

```
rustup default <channel>
```

Overriding Toolchains

Set a specific toolchain for a directory:

```
rustup override set nightly
```

Remove the override:

```
rustup override unset
```

Additional Utilities

rustfmt: Code Formatting

Ensure consistent code style using rustfmt:

```
rustup component add rustfmt
cargo fmt
```

clippy: Linting

Identify potential issues and improve code quality:

```
rustup component add clippy
cargo clippy
```

miri: Code Interpretation

Run and debug unsafe or complex code:

```
rustup component add miri
cargo miri run
```

Customizing the Build Process

The Cargo.toml file allows extensive customization of the build process.

Build Scripts

Use build scripts (build.rs) for custom compilation steps. Example:

```
fn main() {
    println!("cargo:rerun-if-changed=src/main.rs");
```

```
}
```

Profiles

Define custom build profiles for different stages:

```
[profile.dev]
opt-level = 1

[profile.release]
opt-level = 3
```

Debugging and Profiling

Debugging

Use tools like gdb or lldb to debug Rust programs. Compile with debug symbols:

```
cargo build
```

Run the debugger:

```
gdb ./target/debug/my_project
```

Profiling

Analyze performance using perf or similar tools. Compile with optimizations:

```
cargo build --release
```

Summary

The Rust toolchain is a cohesive ecosystem designed for productivity and efficiency. By mastering rustc, cargo, and supplementary tools like rustfmt and clippy, developers can write robust, well-optimized Rust applications. A deep understanding of these tools sets the stage for tackling complex projects and leveraging Rust's full potential.

Chapter 3: Core Concepts of Rust

Ownership and Borrowing

Ownership and borrowing are foundational concepts in Rust, and they distinguish it from many other programming languages. Understanding these principles is essential for mastering Rust and taking full advantage of its safety and performance features. This section delves deep into the mechanisms of ownership and borrowing, exploring their nuances and practical applications.

The Ownership Model in Rust

Rust's ownership model is a set of rules that the compiler enforces to ensure memory safety without needing a garbage collector. The model revolves around three key rules:

1. **Each value in Rust has a variable that's its owner.**
2. **There can only be one owner at a time.**
3. **When the owner goes out of scope, the value is dropped.**

These rules ensure that memory is managed deterministically, and there are no surprises regarding resource allocation and deallocation.

Example: Ownership in Action

```
fn main() {
    let s1 = String::from("hello");
    let s2 = s1; // Ownership is transferred to s2

    // println!("{}", s1); // This would cause a compile-time error
    println!("{}", s2);
}
```

In the above example, ownership of the string s1 is transferred to s2. After this transfer, s1 is no longer valid, and any attempt to use it will result in a compile-time error.

Borrowing: A Safer Way to Use Data

Borrowing allows you to use data without taking ownership. Borrowing is achieved through references, which can be either mutable or immutable:

- **Immutable references**: Allow read-only access to data.
- **Mutable references**: Allow modification of data but come with stricter rules.

Immutable Borrowing

You can create multiple immutable references to the same data, but you cannot modify the data through these references.

```rust
fn main() {
    let s = String::from("hello");

    let r1 = &s;
    let r2 = &s;

    println!("{} and {}", r1, r2);
}
```

Here, r1 and r2 are immutable references to s. This works because Rust ensures that no one can modify s while it's being borrowed immutably.

Mutable Borrowing

Mutable references allow modification of the borrowed data, but only one mutable reference can exist at a time.

```rust
fn main() {
    let mut s = String::from("hello");

    let r1 = &mut s;
    r1.push_str(", world");

    println!("{}", r1);
}
```

This code modifies the string s through the mutable reference r1.

Combining Ownership and Borrowing

Ownership and borrowing work together to prevent common memory errors like null pointer dereferencing, dangling pointers, and data races.

Dangling Pointer Prevention

Rust prevents dangling pointers by enforcing strict ownership and borrowing rules.

```rust
fn main() {
```

```
    let r;

    {
        let x = 5;
        r = &x; // Error: `x` does not live long enough
    }

    println!("{}", r);
}
```

Here, Rust ensures that r cannot reference x because x is dropped at the end of its scope.

Borrow Checker in Action

The borrow checker enforces borrowing rules at compile time, ensuring that data is accessed safely. This prevents errors like use-after-free, where a program tries to access memory that has already been deallocated.

```
fn main() {
    let mut s = String::from("hello");

    let r1 = &s;
    let r2 = &s;
    let r3 = &mut s; // Error: cannot borrow `s` as mutable because
it is also borrowed as immutable

    println!("{}, {}, {}", r1, r2, r3);
}
```

Practical Applications of Ownership and Borrowing

Ownership and borrowing are not just theoretical concepts; they have real-world applications in writing safe and efficient Rust programs.

Function Arguments and Ownership

When passing variables to functions, you can either transfer ownership, borrow immutably, or borrow mutably.

```
fn main() {
    let s = String::from("hello");
```

```rust
    print_string(s); // Ownership is transferred

    // println!("{}", s); // This would cause a compile-time error
}

fn print_string(s: String) {
    println!("{}", s);
}
```

Alternatively, borrowing allows the caller to retain ownership:

```rust
fn main() {
    let s = String::from("hello");
    print_string(&s); // Borrowing

    println!("{}", s); // Ownership is retained
}

fn print_string(s: &String) {
    println!("{}", s);
}
```

Return Values and Ownership

Functions can also return ownership:

```rust
fn main() {
    let s1 = String::from("hello");
    let s2 = take_and_give_back(s1);

    println!("{}", s2);
}

fn take_and_give_back(s: String) -> String {
    s
}
```

This pattern is often used for resource management.

Advanced Borrowing Techniques

Slices and Borrowing

Slices provide a view into a part of a collection, and they work seamlessly with borrowing.

```
fn main() {
    let s = String::from("hello world");

    let word = first_word(&s);

    println!("The first word is: {}", word);
}

fn first_word(s: &String) -> &str {
    let bytes = s.as_bytes();

    for (i, &item) in bytes.iter().enumerate() {
        if item == b' ' {
            return &s[0..i];
        }
    }

    &s[..]
}
```

Borrowing in Loops

Borrowing is often used in loops to iterate over collections without consuming them.

```
fn main() {
    let v = vec![1, 2, 3];

    for item in &v {
        println!("{}", item);
    }

    println!("Vector is still usable: {:?}", v);
}
```

Conclusion

Ownership and borrowing form the backbone of Rust's memory management system. By adhering to the rules enforced by the compiler, developers can write safe and efficient programs without relying on garbage collection. Mastering these concepts is key to harnessing Rust's full potential and writing idiomatic Rust code.

Memory Safety Without Garbage Collection

Memory safety is a cornerstone of Rust's design philosophy. Unlike many modern programming languages, Rust achieves memory safety without relying on a garbage collector. Instead, it uses compile-time checks and its ownership model to ensure that memory is allocated and deallocated correctly. This section explores how Rust ensures memory safety, the benefits of avoiding garbage collection, and practical examples to illustrate these concepts.

The Problem with Garbage Collection

Garbage collection is a common approach to managing memory in programming languages like Java, Python, and Go. While it simplifies memory management for developers, it has notable drawbacks:

1. **Performance Overheads**: Garbage collectors pause program execution to identify and reclaim unused memory, leading to potential latency and jitter.
2. **Unpredictable Timing**: Memory cleanup occurs at indeterminate intervals, which can be problematic for real-time systems or performance-critical applications.
3. **Resource Usage**: Garbage collection algorithms consume additional CPU and memory resources, reducing efficiency.

Rust avoids these issues entirely by employing a deterministic approach to memory management.

Rust's Approach to Memory Safety

Rust provides memory safety through its ownership and borrowing system. These mechanisms allow the compiler to enforce rules that prevent common memory-related errors such as use-after-free, null pointer dereferences, and double frees.

Ownership and Scopes

Every value in Rust has a single owner, and when the owner goes out of scope, the value is automatically deallocated. This eliminates the need for manual memory management or garbage collection.

```
fn main() {
    {
        let x = String::from("hello");
```

```
    println!("{}", x); // x is valid here
} // x is automatically dropped here
}
```

In the above example, x is allocated on the heap when it is created and deallocated automatically when it goes out of scope.

Borrowing and References

Borrowing allows a variable to temporarily share its data without transferring ownership. This ensures that data is not accidentally modified or accessed after it has been deallocated.

Immutable References

Immutable references let you read data without modifying it. Multiple immutable references can coexist.

```
fn main() {
    let s = String::from("Rust");

    let r1 = &s;
    let r2 = &s;

    println!("{} and {}", r1, r2); // Both references are valid
}
```

Mutable References

A mutable reference allows modification of data but is limited to one active mutable reference at a time.

```
fn main() {
    let mut s = String::from("Rust");

    let r = &mut s;
    r.push_str(" programming");

    println!("{}", r);
}
```

Preventing Null and Dangling Pointers

Rust does not have null references. Instead, it uses the `Option` type to represent optional values explicitly.

```rust
fn main() {
    let some_number: Option<i32> = Some(42);
    let no_number: Option<i32> = None;

    match some_number {
        Some(value) => println!("Number is: {}", value),
        None => println!("No number"),
    }
}
```

The absence of null references eliminates null pointer dereferencing, a common source of bugs in languages like C and C++.

Similarly, Rust prevents dangling pointers by ensuring that references are valid for the lifetime of the data they point to.

```rust
fn main() {
    let r;
    {
        let x = 10;
        r = &x; // Error: x does not live long enough
    }
    println!("{}", r);
}
```

Benefits of Rust's Approach

By enforcing memory safety at compile time, Rust offers several advantages:

1. **Performance**: Without the need for garbage collection, Rust programs run with predictable performance and low latency.
2. **Safety**: Compile-time checks prevent memory-related bugs, leading to more robust programs.
3. **Control**: Developers have fine-grained control over memory allocation and deallocation, making Rust ideal for systems programming.

Practical Applications of Memory Safety

Building Reliable Systems

Rust's memory safety guarantees make it suitable for building reliable systems, such as operating systems, embedded software, and real-time applications.

```rust
fn allocate_buffer(size: usize) -> Vec<u8> {
    let buffer = vec![0; size]; // Memory is allocated here
    buffer // Ownership is returned
}

fn main() {
    let buffer = allocate_buffer(1024);
    println!("Buffer size: {}", buffer.len());
} // Buffer is automatically deallocated here
```

Concurrency Without Data Races

Rust prevents data races at compile time by enforcing strict ownership and borrowing rules in multithreaded contexts.

```rust
use std::thread;

fn main() {
    let mut data = vec![1, 2, 3];

    let handle = thread::spawn(move || {
        data.push(4); // Ownership is moved to the thread
    });

    handle.join().unwrap();
}
```

In this example, ownership of data is transferred to the thread, ensuring that no other part of the program can access it simultaneously.

Efficient Resource Management

Rust's deterministic memory management ensures efficient use of resources, making it ideal for embedded systems and resource-constrained environments.

```rust
fn main() {
    let sensor_data = vec![1.0, 2.0, 3.0];
```

```
    process_data(&sensor_data); // Borrowing avoids copying

    println!("Sensor data: {:?}", sensor_data); // Still accessible
}

fn process_data(data: &Vec<f64>) {
    for value in data {
        println!("Processing: {}", value);
    }
}
```

Challenges and Best Practices

While Rust's memory safety model eliminates many classes of bugs, it comes with a learning curve. Adhering to best practices can help developers write idiomatic and efficient Rust code:

1. **Understand Ownership**: Familiarize yourself with ownership, borrowing, and lifetimes.
2. **Use the Borrow Checker**: Let the borrow checker guide you in resolving borrowing conflicts.
3. **Leverage Rust's Standard Library**: Use abstractions like `Rc` and `Arc` for shared ownership when necessary.
4. **Profile and Optimize**: Use tools like `cargo build --release` and `cargo profiler` to optimize performance.

Conclusion

Rust's approach to memory safety without garbage collection represents a paradigm shift in programming. By leveraging ownership, borrowing, and strict compile-time checks, Rust enables developers to write safe, high-performance code. Understanding and applying these principles is key to mastering Rust and unlocking its full potential.

Data Types and Pattern Matching

Rust is a strongly-typed programming language, which means every value in Rust has a specific data type known at compile time. This ensures type safety and enables powerful features like pattern matching. In this section, we will delve into the core data types in Rust, their practical applications, and how pattern matching enhances control flow and error handling in Rust programs.

Core Data Types in Rust

Rust's data types can be broadly categorized into scalar types, compound types, and custom types.

Scalar Types

Scalar types represent a single value. Rust provides several scalar types:

1. **Integer Types**: Signed (`i8`, `i16`, `i32`, `i64`, `i128`, `isize`) and unsigned (`u8`, `u16`, `u32`, `u64`, `u128`, `usize`).
2. **Floating-Point Types**: `f32` and `f64` for single and double precision.
3. **Boolean Type**: `bool` with values `true` and `false`.
4. **Character Type**: `char` for Unicode scalar values.

Example: Using Scalar Types

```
fn main() {
    let integer: i32 = 42;
    let floating_point: f64 = 3.14;
    let boolean: bool = true;
    let character: char = 'R';

    println!("Integer: {}", integer);
    println!("Floating Point: {}", floating_point);
    println!("Boolean: {}", boolean);
    println!("Character: {}", character);
}
```

Compound Types

Compound types group multiple values into one type. Rust supports two primary compound types:

1. **Tuples**: Fixed-size collections of multiple types.
2. **Arrays**: Fixed-size collections of values of the same type.

Example: Tuples

```
fn main() {
    let person: (&str, i32, f64) = ("Alice", 30, 5.4);
    let (name, age, height) = person;

    println!("Name: {}, Age: {}, Height: {}", name, age, height);
}
```

Example: Arrays

```
fn main() {
```

```rust
    let numbers: [i32; 4] = [1, 2, 3, 4];

    for num in numbers.iter() {
        println!("{}", num);
    }
}
```

Custom Types

Rust allows the creation of custom types using structures, enumerations, and type aliases.

Structs

Structures (`struct`) define custom data types with named fields.

```rust
struct Point {
    x: f64,
    y: f64,
}

fn main() {
    let point = Point { x: 3.0, y: 4.0 };
    println!("Point coordinates: ({}, {})", point.x, point.y);
}
```

Enums

Enumerations (`enum`) define types that can be one of several variants.

```rust
enum Direction {
    Up,
    Down,
    Left,
    Right,
}

fn main() {
    let direction = Direction::Up;

    match direction {
        Direction::Up => println!("Going up!"),
```

```
        Direction::Down => println!("Going down!"),
        Direction::Left => println!("Turning left!"),
        Direction::Right => println!("Turning right!"),
    }
}
```

Pattern Matching in Rust

Pattern matching is a powerful feature in Rust, enabling concise and expressive handling of data structures and control flow. The match expression is the cornerstone of pattern matching in Rust, and it works alongside other constructs like if let and while let.

The match Expression

The match expression allows branching based on patterns. Each pattern is evaluated in sequence until a match is found.

Example: Matching Values

```
fn main() {
    let number = 3;

    match number {
        1 => println!("One"),
        2 => println!("Two"),
        3 => println!("Three"),
        _ => println!("Something else"),
    }
}
```

The _ wildcard pattern matches any value not explicitly handled.

Matching with Enums

Pattern matching works seamlessly with enums, making it easy to handle different variants.

```
enum Result {
    Success(i32),
    Failure(String),
}

fn main() {
```

```rust
    let result = Result::Success(42);

    match result {
        Result::Success(value) => println!("Success with value: {}",
value),
        Result::Failure(error) => println!("Failure: {}", error),
    }
}
```

Destructuring in Patterns

Rust's pattern matching supports destructuring, allowing you to extract values from tuples, arrays, and structs.

Example: Destructuring Tuples

```rust
fn main() {
    let coordinates = (3, 4);

    match coordinates {
        (x, y) => println!("x: {}, y: {}", x, y),
    }
}
```

Example: Destructuring Structs

```rust
struct Point {
    x: i32,
    y: i32,
}

fn main() {
    let point = Point { x: 10, y: 20 };

    match point {
        Point { x, y } => println!("Point is at ({}, {})", x, y),
    }
}
```

Advanced Pattern Matching

Matching Ranges

You can match values against ranges using the ..= operator.

```
fn main() {
    let score = 85;

    match score {
        0..=49 => println!("Fail"),
        50..=74 => println!("Pass"),
        75..=100 => println!("Distinction"),
        _ => println!("Invalid score"),
    }
}
```

Combining Patterns

Patterns can be combined using the | operator.

```
fn main() {
    let day = "Saturday";

    match day {
        "Saturday" | "Sunday" => println!("Weekend!"),
        _ => println!("Weekday"),
    }
}
```

Conditional Matching

You can add conditions to patterns using if.

```
fn main() {
    let number = 42;

    match number {
        x if x % 2 == 0 => println!("Even number: {}", x),
        _ => println!("Odd number"),
    }
}
```

Pattern Matching in Error Handling

Pattern matching is extensively used in Rust's error handling with the `Result` and `Option` types.

Matching `Result`

```rust
fn divide(a: i32, b: i32) -> Result<i32, String> {
    if b == 0 {
        Err(String::from("Division by zero"))
    } else {
        Ok(a / b)
    }
}

fn main() {
    let result = divide(10, 2);

    match result {
        Ok(value) => println!("Result: {}", value),
        Err(error) => println!("Error: {}", error),
    }
}
```

Matching `Option`

```rust
fn main() {
    let value: Option<i32> = Some(5);

    match value {
        Some(x) => println!("Value: {}", x),
        None => println!("No value"),
    }
}
```

Conclusion

Understanding Rust's data types and pattern matching is essential for writing efficient and expressive code. Rust's strong typing ensures safety and correctness, while pattern matching provides a versatile and powerful mechanism for handling complex data and control flow. By mastering these concepts, you can write clean, idiomatic, and robust Rust programs.

Chapter 4: Building Blocks of Rust Programs

Variables, Constants, and Mutability

Understanding variables, constants, and mutability is fundamental to mastering Rust's programming paradigm. Rust provides a powerful type system and a unique approach to memory safety, which makes managing variables and constants a crucial skill for any developer.

Variables in Rust

In Rust, variables are immutable by default. This design enforces safety and prevents accidental modification of values, which is common in many programming languages.

```
fn main() {
    let x = 5; // Immutable variable
    println!("The value of x is: {}", x);

    // Uncommenting the following line will result in a compile-time
error:
    // x = 6; // Error: cannot assign twice to immutable variable `x`
}
```

If you need a variable that can be modified, Rust allows you to explicitly declare it as mutable using the mut keyword:

```
fn main() {
    let mut y = 10; // Mutable variable
    println!("The initial value of y is: {}", y);

    y = 15; // Reassigning a new value
    println!("The updated value of y is: {}", y);
}
```

By making immutability the default, Rust encourages developers to write safer and more predictable code.

Constants

Constants are always immutable, and their value must be set at compile time. They are declared using the const keyword and must have a type explicitly specified. Constants are commonly used for values that remain unchanged throughout the program's lifetime, such as configuration parameters.

```
const MAX_POINTS: u32 = 100_000;

fn main() {
    println!("The maximum points are: {}", MAX_POINTS);
}
```

Unlike variables, constants can be declared in any scope, including outside functions, making them accessible globally.

Shadowing

Rust allows you to declare a new variable with the same name as a previous variable, effectively "shadowing" the old variable. This is useful when you want to perform transformations on a value without creating additional variable names.

```
fn main() {
    let x = 5;
    let x = x + 1;
    let x = x * 2;

    println!("The final value of x is: {}", x);
}
```

Shadowing is different from marking a variable as mut because the type of the variable can also change during shadowing.

```
fn main() {
    let spaces = "    ";
    let spaces = spaces.len(); // Shadowed with a different type
    println!("The number of spaces is: {}", spaces);
}
```

Type Annotations

Rust can infer the type of a variable based on its value, but you can also specify it explicitly:

```
fn main() {
    let guess: u32 = "42".parse().expect("Not a number!");
    println!("Your guess is: {}", guess);
}
```

Explicit type annotations are useful in scenarios where type inference is ambiguous or when working with complex types.

Constants vs. Immutable Variables

While both constants and immutable variables cannot be changed, there are key differences:

- Constants are declared using const and must have an explicit type.
- Constants are evaluated at compile time and cannot be the result of a runtime computation.
- Constants have a broader scope and can be used anywhere, even outside functions.

```
const SECONDS_IN_MINUTE: u32 = 60;

fn main() {
    let minutes = 5;
    let seconds = minutes * SECONDS_IN_MINUTE;
    println!("{} minutes is {} seconds.", minutes, seconds);
}
```

Mutability and Safety

The explicit mut keyword helps developers distinguish between mutable and immutable data, reducing unintended side effects. However, mutability in Rust is carefully controlled to prevent data races in concurrent programming. This design principle aligns with Rust's emphasis on safety and performance.

```
fn main() {
    let mut counter = 0;

    for _ in 0..10 {
        counter += 1;
    }

    println!("The counter value is: {}", counter);
```

```
}
```

Performance Considerations

Rust's emphasis on immutability and explicit mutability has performance implications. Immutable variables enable the compiler to perform aggressive optimizations, such as constant folding and inlining. By minimizing mutable variables, developers can leverage these optimizations to write highly efficient code.

Best Practices

1. **Favor Immutability:** Use immutable variables unless mutability is absolutely necessary. This leads to safer and more maintainable code.
2. **Use Constants for Global Values:** Declare constants for values that do not change and are reused in multiple places.
3. **Avoid Overusing `mut`:** Limit the scope and use of mutable variables to ensure clarity and reduce potential errors.
4. **Leverage Shadowing:** Use shadowing to transform data while maintaining immutability.

Exercises

1. Declare a constant for the number of hours in a day and use it to calculate the total minutes in a week.
2. Write a program that demonstrates shadowing by converting a string to its length.
3. Create a mutable variable to count the number of iterations in a loop and print the count.

By mastering variables, constants, and mutability, you lay a solid foundation for building robust and efficient Rust programs. This understanding is essential as you delve deeper into Rust's advanced features and its unique approach to system-level programming.

Functions and Modules

Functions and modules are core components of Rust's design, allowing developers to write modular, reusable, and maintainable code. This section explores these concepts in depth, covering everything from basic function definitions to advanced module organization.

Functions in Rust

Functions in Rust are defined using the `fn` keyword, followed by the function name, a set of parentheses (which may include parameters), and a block of code. The following is a simple example:

```
fn main() {
```

```
    greet();
}

fn greet() {
    println!("Hello, world!");
}
```

Here, the greet function is defined separately and then called from the main function.

Function Parameters

Functions in Rust can accept parameters. You must specify the type of each parameter explicitly, as Rust does not allow implicit type inference for function parameters.

```
fn main() {
    print_sum(5, 10);
}

fn print_sum(x: i32, y: i32) {
    println!("The sum of {} and {} is {}", x, y, x + y);
}
```

In this example, x and y are parameters of type i32. When calling print_sum, we pass two integers as arguments.

Return Values

Functions can return values using the -> syntax to specify the return type. The return value is the last expression in the function, and it does not require a return keyword unless explicitly needed.

```
fn main() {
    let result = add(5, 10);
    println!("The result is {}", result);
}

fn add(a: i32, b: i32) -> i32 {
    a + b
}
```

Here, the `add` function returns the sum of `a` and `b`. Note that the last expression does not include a semicolon, which differentiates it from a statement.

The `return` Keyword

While most Rust functions return the last expression, you can use the `return` keyword to return a value earlier in the function.

```rust
fn main() {
    let value = conditional_return(true);
    println!("The value is {}", value);
}

fn conditional_return(condition: bool) -> i32 {
    if condition {
        return 42;
    }
    0
}
```

Nested Functions

Rust does not support defining functions inside other functions directly, but you can achieve similar behavior using closures or modules, which we will explore later.

Modules in Rust

Modules are Rust's way of organizing code into logical units, enabling reusability and clarity. A module can contain functions, structs, enums, constants, and even other modules.

Declaring a Module

A module is declared using the `mod` keyword. Its contents can be defined inline or in a separate file.

```rust
mod math {
    pub fn add(a: i32, b: i32) -> i32 {
        a + b
    }
}

fn main() {
```

```
    let sum = math::add(5, 10);
    println!("The sum is {}", sum);
}
```

Here, the math module contains an add function, which is marked as pub to make it public and accessible outside the module.

Nested Modules

Modules can be nested to create a hierarchical structure.

```
mod library {
    pub mod math {
        pub fn multiply(a: i32, b: i32) -> i32 {
            a * b
        }
    }
}

fn main() {
    let product = library::math::multiply(4, 5);
    println!("The product is {}", product);
}
```

Module Files

For larger projects, Rust allows you to define modules in separate files. For example, if you create a math.rs file, it can act as the math module.

```
// math.rs
pub fn subtract(a: i32, b: i32) -> i32 {
    a - b
}

// main.rs
mod math;

fn main() {
    let difference = math::subtract(10, 4);
    println!("The difference is {}", difference);
```

```
}
```

Using use for Convenience

To simplify access to items in a module, you can use the use keyword:

```rust
mod library {
    pub mod math {
        pub fn divide(a: i32, b: i32) -> i32 {
            a / b
        }
    }
}

use library::math::divide;

fn main() {
    let quotient = divide(20, 4);
    println!("The quotient is {}", quotient);
}
```

Combining Functions and Modules

Functions and modules work seamlessly together to create organized and reusable code structures. For example:

```rust
mod utilities {
    pub fn greet_user(name: &str) {
        println!("Hello, {}!", name);
    }

    pub fn calculate_square(num: i32) -> i32 {
        num * num
    }
}

fn main() {
    utilities::greet_user("Alice");
    let square = utilities::calculate_square(6);
    println!("The square of 6 is {}", square);
```

```
}
```

Best Practices for Functions and Modules

1. **Use Descriptive Names:** Functions and modules should have names that clearly indicate their purpose.
2. **Limit Function Length:** Keep functions short and focused on a single task.
3. **Encapsulate Logic:** Use modules to encapsulate related functions and data, reducing global scope pollution.
4. **Document Your Code:** Use comments or Rust's documentation tools to explain the purpose of functions and modules.

Exercises

1. Write a module named `geometry` containing functions to calculate the area of a circle and the perimeter of a rectangle. Use the module in your `main` function.
2. Create a nested module structure for a `store` application. Include functions for adding and removing items from an inventory.
3. Refactor a large function into multiple smaller functions organized within a module for clarity and reusability.

By mastering functions and modules, you gain the tools to write structured, maintainable, and efficient Rust programs. These building blocks will serve you well as you tackle more complex projects and advanced features.

Control Flow and Error Handling

Control flow and error handling are fundamental aspects of programming that dictate how your application processes logic and handles unexpected situations. Rust provides robust constructs for control flow, ensuring clarity and safety in decision-making and error management.

Control Flow in Rust

Rust supports the traditional control flow structures such as `if`, `else`, `match`, `loop`, `while`, and `for`. These structures enable developers to create flexible and expressive logic in their programs.

`if` and `else` Statements

Rust's `if` statements are straightforward and similar to other languages, but they must always evaluate to a `bool`.

```
fn main() {
```

```
    let number = 7;

    if number < 10 {
        println!("The number is less than 10.");
    } else {
        println!("The number is 10 or greater.");
    }
}
```

In Rust, if is an expression, which means it can return a value. This allows for concise logic when initializing variables:

```
fn main() {
    let condition = true;
    let number = if condition { 5 } else { 10 };

    println!("The value of number is: {}", number);
}
```

match for Pattern Matching

The match statement is a powerful control flow construct that allows you to match patterns against a value. It's particularly useful for handling enums and other structured data.

```
fn main() {
    let coin = "penny";

    let value = match coin {
        "penny" => 1,
        "nickel" => 5,
        "dime" => 10,
        "quarter" => 25,
        _ => 0, // The catch-all pattern
    };

    println!("The value of the coin is: {}", value);
}
```

The _ pattern acts as a wildcard, ensuring all possible values are handled.

Loops

Rust provides several looping constructs:

1. `loop`: An infinite loop that runs until explicitly exited with a `break` statement.

```rust
fn main() {
    let mut count = 0;

    loop {
        count += 1;

        if count == 5 {
            break;
        }

        println!("Count is: {}", count);
    }
}
```

2. `while`: Runs as long as a condition evaluates to `true`.

```rust
fn main() {
    let mut number = 3;

    while number != 0 {
        println!("{}", number);
        number -= 1;
    }

    println!("Liftoff!");
}
```

3. `for`: Iterates over a range or collection.

```rust
fn main() {
    for number in 1..5 {
        println!("Number: {}", number);
    }
```

```
}
```

Iterating Over Collections

Using `for` loops to iterate over collections like arrays or vectors is idiomatic in Rust.

```rust
fn main() {
    let numbers = [10, 20, 30, 40];

    for num in numbers.iter() {
        println!("The number is: {}", num);
    }
}
```

Error Handling in Rust

Rust emphasizes safety, and its error handling mechanisms reflect this priority. It distinguishes between recoverable and unrecoverable errors.

Recoverable Errors: The `Result` Type

Rust's `Result` type is used for operations that might fail but are expected to be handled by the programmer.

```rust
use std::fs::File;

fn main() {
    let file = File::open("hello.txt");

    let file = match file {
        Ok(f) => f,
        Err(error) => {
            println!("Error opening file: {:?}", error);
            return;
        },
    };

    println!("File opened successfully.");
}
```

The Result type has two variants:

- Ok(value): Indicates success, wrapping the resulting value.
- Err(error): Indicates failure, wrapping an error value.

Propagating Errors with the ? Operator

The ? operator simplifies error propagation, allowing you to delegate error handling to the caller.

```rust
use std::fs::File;
use std::io::{self, Read};

fn read_file() -> io::Result<String> {
    let mut file = File::open("hello.txt")?;
    let mut contents = String::new();
    file.read_to_string(&mut contents)?;
    Ok(contents)
}

fn main() {
    match read_file() {
        Ok(contents) => println!("File contents: {}", contents),
        Err(e) => println!("Error reading file: {:?}", e),
    }
}
```

Here, the ? operator returns early if an error occurs, simplifying the code.

Unrecoverable Errors: The panic! Macro

Rust's panic! macro is used to handle unrecoverable errors by terminating the program.

```rust
fn main() {
    panic!("This is a critical error!");
}
```

Panic should be used sparingly, as it abruptly ends the program, which may not be desirable in all situations.

Custom Error Types

For complex applications, you can define custom error types to provide more context when errors occur.

```rust
#[derive(Debug)]
enum CustomError {
    FileNotFound,
    InvalidData,
}

fn example_function() -> Result<(), CustomError> {
    Err(CustomError::FileNotFound)
}

fn main() {
    match example_function() {
        Ok(_) => println!("Operation succeeded."),
        Err(e) => println!("Error occurred: {:?}", e),
    }
}
```

Combining Control Flow and Error Handling

Control flow constructs and error handling often work together to manage complex logic.

```rust
use std::fs::File;

fn main() {
    let file = File::open("config.txt");

    match file {
        Ok(_) => println!("File opened successfully."),
        Err(error) => {
            if error.kind() == std::io::ErrorKind::NotFound {
                println!("File not found. Creating a new file...");
            } else {
                println!("Error opening file: {:?}", error);
            }
        },
    }
}
```

Best Practices

1. **Handle All Possible Cases:** Use `match` or _ patterns to ensure all scenarios are covered.
2. **Use `Result` for Recoverable Errors:** Avoid using `panic!` for errors that can be handled gracefully.
3. **Leverage the `?` Operator:** Simplify error propagation when appropriate.
4. **Keep Loops Readable:** Avoid deeply nested logic within loops to maintain code clarity.

Exercises

1. Write a program that reads a number from the user and determines whether it is even or odd using `if` and `else`.
2. Create a function that calculates the factorial of a number using a `for` loop.
3. Implement a file reader that handles errors gracefully, creating a file if it does not exist.
4. Use the `match` statement to handle different types of coins and print their values.

Control flow and error handling are essential tools for creating robust Rust programs. By mastering these concepts, you can write code that is not only efficient but also resilient to unexpected conditions.

Chapter 5: Mastering the Borrow Checker

Lifetimes and Scopes

Understanding lifetimes and scopes is a crucial aspect of mastering Rust's ownership and borrowing model. At its core, lifetimes ensure that references in Rust are valid as long as they are needed but no longer. This section delves deep into lifetimes and scopes, providing a comprehensive guide for navigating Rust's stringent yet empowering borrow checker.

The Need for Lifetimes

Rust's ownership model emphasizes safety and concurrency without a garbage collector. Lifetimes are a way to inform the Rust compiler about the scope within which references are valid. This ensures that there are no dangling references or use-after-free errors in your programs.

Consider this simple example:

```
fn main() {
    let r;
    {
        let x = 5;
        r = &x;
    } // x goes out of scope here
    println!("{}", r); // Error: `r` references a value out of scope
}
```

In the above code, the reference r is tied to x, which goes out of scope before r is used. Lifetimes allow Rust to detect such issues at compile time.

Lifetime Annotations

Lifetime annotations are represented using an apostrophe followed by a name (e.g., 'a). They explicitly specify how long references live relative to one another. For example:

```
fn longest<'a>(x: &'a str, y: &'a str) -> &'a str {
    if x.len() > y.len() {
        x
    } else {
        y
    }
}
```

```
}
```

Here:

- `'a` is a lifetime parameter that ensures both input references (x and y) and the return value share the same lifetime.

Example Usage:

```
fn main() {
    let string1 = String::from("long string");
    let string2 = "short";
    let result = longest(string1.as_str(), string2);
    println!("The longest string is {}", result);
}
```

In this example, the `longest` function will only compile if the lifetimes of the inputs allow the result to be valid.

Lifetimes in Structs

You can also use lifetimes in structs to ensure the struct does not outlive its references:

```
struct ImportantExcerpt<'a> {
    part: &'a str,
}

fn main() {
    let novel = String::from("Call me Ishmael. Some years ago...");
    let first_sentence = novel.split('.').next().expect("Could not
find a '.'");
    let excerpt = ImportantExcerpt {
        part: first_sentence,
    };
    println!("Excerpt: {}", excerpt.part);
}
```

Here, the struct `ImportantExcerpt` has a lifetime annotation to indicate that its field `part` cannot outlive the reference it borrows.

Elision Rules

Rust has rules for lifetime elision, which allow omitting lifetime annotations in some cases. The compiler infers the lifetimes based on these rules:

1. Each parameter with a reference gets its own lifetime.
2. If there is one input lifetime, it is assigned to all output lifetimes.
3. If there are multiple input lifetimes, but one of them is &self or &mut self, the output lifetime is assigned to self.

For example, these two functions are equivalent:

Without Elision:

```
fn first_word<'a>(s: &'a str) -> &'a str {
    s.split_whitespace().next().unwrap()
}
```

With Elision:

```
fn first_word(s: &str) -> &str {
    s.split_whitespace().next().unwrap()
}
```

Scopes and Lifetimes

Scopes determine how long a variable, reference, or resource is valid. Lifetimes ensure that references do not outlive the scope they are tied to.

Consider this example of nested scopes:

```
fn main() {
    let outer;
    {
        let inner = String::from("hello");
        outer = &inner;
    } // `inner` is dropped here
    println!("{}", outer); // Compile-time error
}
```

The Rust compiler prevents outer from referencing inner after inner has gone out of scope.

Static Lifetimes

A `'static` lifetime refers to the entire duration of the program. All string literals, for instance, have a `'static` lifetime:

```
fn main() {
    let s: &'static str = "I have a static lifetime.";
    println!("{}", s);
}
```

Be cautious when using `'static` lifetimes with non-constant data, as it may lead to memory leaks if misused.

Common Borrowing Pitfalls and Solutions

1. Dangling References

This occurs when a reference outlives the data it points to. Rust prevents this at compile time.

2. Mutable and Immutable Borrowing

You cannot borrow a value mutably and immutably at the same time:

```
fn main() {
    let mut s = String::from("hello");
    let r1 = &s;
    let r2 = &mut s; // Error
    println!("{}, {}", r1, r2);
}
```

Solution: Limit the lifetime of immutable borrows before creating a mutable one.

3. Lifetime Ambiguities

Complex functions may require explicitly annotated lifetimes to resolve ambiguities.

Leveraging the Borrow Checker

The borrow checker ensures that your code adheres to Rust's safety guarantees. By understanding lifetimes and scopes, you can design APIs and data structures that are safe and efficient.

Example: A Safe Resource Manager

```rust
struct Resource<'a> {
    data: &'a str,
}

impl<'a> Resource<'a> {
    fn new(data: &'a str) -> Self {
        Resource { data }
    }

    fn get_data(&self) -> &str {
        self.data
    }
}

fn main() {
    let data = String::from("Resource data");
    let manager = Resource::new(&data);
    println!("Managed data: {}", manager.get_data());
}
```

This example demonstrates how lifetimes ensure that the `Resource` struct cannot outlive the data it manages.

Summary

Lifetimes and scopes form the backbone of Rust's memory safety guarantees. By mastering these concepts, you can write robust and efficient programs, leveraging the borrow checker as a guide rather than an obstacle. The careful use of lifetime annotations, understanding of scopes, and adherence to borrowing rules will empower you to create complex yet safe systems in Rust.

Avoiding Common Borrowing Pitfalls

Borrowing is one of the foundational principles of Rust's ownership model. It allows you to use references to data without transferring ownership. However, improper borrowing can lead to compile-time errors, making it essential to understand and avoid common pitfalls. In this section, we will explore frequent borrowing mistakes and provide practical solutions to overcome them.

Understanding Borrowing Rules

Before diving into the pitfalls, it's essential to recap Rust's borrowing rules:

1. At any time, you can have **either** one mutable reference **or** any number of immutable references to a piece of data.
2. References must always be valid, meaning they cannot outlive the data they point to.

Example of Proper Borrowing:

```
fn main() {
    let data = String::from("hello");
    let ref1 = &data; // Immutable borrow
    let ref2 = &data; // Another immutable borrow
    println!("{}, {}", ref1, ref2); // Both references can be used

    let mut data = String::from("hello");
    let ref_mut = &mut data; // Mutable borrow
    ref_mut.push_str(", world");
    println!("{}", ref_mut); // Mutable borrow is valid here
}
```

Pitfall 1: Dangling References

A dangling reference occurs when a reference points to data that has been dropped. Rust prevents this by ensuring that references are always valid.

Example of a Dangling Reference:

```
fn dangling_reference() -> &String {
    let s = String::from("hello");
    &s // Error: `s` is dropped at the end of this function
}
```

Solution:

Move the ownership of the data or return the data itself:

```
fn valid_reference() -> String {
    let s = String::from("hello");
    s // Ownership is moved, no dangling reference
}
```

Pitfall 2: Mutable and Immutable Borrowing Conflict

Attempting to borrow a value as mutable while it is already borrowed as immutable will result in a compile-time error.

Problematic Example:

```
fn main() {
    let mut data = String::from("hello");
    let ref1 = &data; // Immutable borrow
    let ref2 = &mut data; // Error: Cannot borrow as mutable while
immutable borrow exists
    println!("{}, {}", ref1, ref2);
}
```

Solution:

Limit the scope of the immutable borrow so that the mutable borrow occurs afterward:

```
fn main() {
    let mut data = String::from("hello");
    {
        let ref1 = &data; // Immutable borrow
        println!("{}", ref1); // Use the immutable reference
    } // ref1 goes out of scope here
    let ref2 = &mut data; // Now mutable borrow is allowed
    ref2.push_str(", world");
    println!("{}", ref2);
}
```

Pitfall 3: Borrowing Across Function Boundaries

Borrowing data and passing it across function boundaries can lead to lifetimes that the compiler cannot resolve.

Example of Borrowing Issue:

```
fn main() {
    let data = String::from("hello");
    let ref_to_data = take_and_return(&data);
    println!("{}", ref_to_data); // Error: `data` might be invalid
}

fn take_and_return(s: &String) -> &String {
```

```
    s // The lifetime of `s` is ambiguous
}
```

Solution:

Use explicit lifetime annotations:

```
fn main() {
    let data = String::from("hello");
    let ref_to_data = take_and_return(&data);
    println!("{}", ref_to_data);
}

fn take_and_return<'a>(s: &'a String) -> &'a String {
    s // Lifetime of `s` is tied to the input
}
```

Pitfall 4: Misunderstanding Lifetime Elision

Lifetime elision rules help avoid excessive annotation, but sometimes explicit lifetimes are required. Misinterpreting the elision can lead to compile-time errors.

Example Requiring Lifetime Annotation:

```
fn first_word(s: &str) -> &str {
    s.split_whitespace().next().unwrap() // Error without lifetime
annotation
}
```

Solution:

Add explicit lifetime annotations:

```
fn first_word<'a>(s: &'a str) -> &'a str {
    s.split_whitespace().next().unwrap()
}
```

Pitfall 5: Borrow Checker Complaints in Loops

Loops often involve borrowing variables, which can clash with mutable borrows or ownership transfers within the same loop.

Problematic Example:

```
fn main() {
    let mut data = vec![1, 2, 3];
    for i in &data {
        data.push(*i); // Error: Cannot borrow `data` as mutable
    }
}
```

Solution:

Use ownership instead of borrowing in loops:

```
fn main() {
    let mut data = vec![1, 2, 3];
    let new_data: Vec<_> = data.iter().map(|&x| x * 2).collect();
    data.extend(new_data);
    println!("{:?}", data);
}
```

Pitfall 6: Borrowing and Closures

Closures can capture references, leading to borrowing conflicts when trying to mutate or use the original variable.

Example:

```
fn main() {
    let mut data = String::from("hello");
    let closure = || {
        println!("{}", data); // Immutable borrow
    };
    data.push_str(", world"); // Error: Cannot borrow as mutable
    closure();
}
```

Solution:

Drop the closure before the mutable borrow or use ownership:

```
fn main() {
    let mut data = String::from("hello");
    {
        let closure = || {
            println!("{}", data); // Immutable borrow
        };
        closure();
    }
    data.push_str(", world"); // Now mutable borrow is allowed
    println!("{}", data);
}
```

Best Practices for Avoiding Borrowing Pitfalls

1. **Plan Reference Lifetimes**: Understand how long each reference will live and limit their scopes accordingly.
2. **Avoid Complex Borrowing in Loops**: Where possible, use owned data instead of references within loops.
3. **Use Lifetimes Explicitly**: When dealing with multiple references, explicitly annotate lifetimes to avoid ambiguity.
4. **Encapsulate Borrowing Logic**: Use structs or helper functions to manage borrowing and lifetimes explicitly.
5. **Leverage the Borrow Checker**: Treat borrow checker errors as opportunities to write safer code rather than obstacles.

Summary

Avoiding borrowing pitfalls requires a clear understanding of Rust's ownership and borrowing model. By recognizing common mistakes and implementing these solutions, you can write efficient, safe, and reliable Rust programs. The borrow checker, while strict, acts as a helpful guide, ensuring your code remains free from runtime memory errors.

Leveraging the Borrow Checker for Better Design

The Rust borrow checker is often perceived as a hurdle for beginners, but its true power lies in guiding developers toward writing better, safer, and more efficient code. By leveraging the borrow checker, you can design programs that are free from common issues such as null pointer dereferences, data races, and memory leaks. This section explores how to use the borrow checker to create clean and robust designs.

The Philosophy Behind the Borrow Checker

The borrow checker enforces strict rules to ensure memory safety. At a high level, its purpose is to:

1. Prevent data races in concurrent programming.
2. Avoid dangling pointers and null references.
3. Encourage immutability wherever possible for predictable and thread-safe code.

By understanding its rules and limitations, you can use the borrow checker as a tool for enhancing your software design.

Borrow Checker in Action: Immutable and Mutable References

The borrow checker enforces the rule that a piece of data can have multiple immutable references or one mutable reference, but not both simultaneously. This principle ensures that no two parts of the program can modify the same data concurrently.

Example of Proper Reference Usage:

```
fn main() {
    let mut numbers = vec![1, 2, 3];

    // Immutable borrow
    let first = &numbers[0];
    println!("First element: {}", first);

    // Mutable borrow
    let last = numbers.last_mut();
    if let Some(value) = last {
        *value += 10;
    }
    println!("Updated vector: {:?}", numbers);
}
```

The borrow checker ensures that the immutable borrow `first` is no longer used when the mutable borrow `last` is introduced.

Designing APIs with Borrowing in Mind

When designing APIs, it is important to leverage borrowing to ensure safe access to resources. This makes the API predictable and prevents misuse.

Example: A Safe Database Wrapper

```
struct Database {
    data: Vec<String>,
```

```rust
}

impl Database {
    fn new() -> Self {
        Database { data: vec![] }
    }

    fn add_entry(&mut self, entry: String) {
        self.data.push(entry);
    }

    fn get_entry(&self, index: usize) -> Option<&String> {
        self.data.get(index)
    }
}

fn main() {
    let mut db = Database::new();
    db.add_entry("First entry".to_string());
    db.add_entry("Second entry".to_string());

    if let Some(entry) = db.get_entry(0) {
        println!("Retrieved entry: {}", entry);
    }
}
```

The Database struct ensures safe access to its internal data by clearly separating mutable and immutable operations. The borrow checker enforces these rules at compile time.

Borrow Checker and Lifetimes

Lifetimes are an integral part of the borrow checker, helping you manage how long references are valid. By explicitly specifying lifetimes, you can design functions and structs that are both flexible and safe.

Example: Struct with Lifetimes

```rust
struct Config<'a> {
    key: &'a str,
    value: &'a str,
}
```

```rust
impl<'a> Config<'a> {
    fn new(key: &'a str, value: &'a str) -> Self {
        Config { key, value }
    }

    fn display(&self) {
        println!("{}: {}", self.key, self.value);
    }
}

fn main() {
    let key = String::from("username");
    let value = String::from("admin");
    let config = Config::new(&key, &value);
    config.display();
}
```

In this example, the lifetime annotations ensure that the `Config` struct does not outlive the references it holds.

Concurrency and the Borrow Checker

The borrow checker plays a vital role in ensuring thread safety in concurrent programs. By enforcing borrowing rules, it prevents data races.

Example: Using `Arc` and `Mutex`

```rust
use std::sync::{Arc, Mutex};
use std::thread;

fn main() {
    let data = Arc::new(Mutex::new(vec![1, 2, 3]));

    let mut handles = vec![];

    for i in 0..3 {
        let data = Arc::clone(&data);
        let handle = thread::spawn(move || {
            let mut vec = data.lock().unwrap();
            vec.push(i);
        });
        handles.push(handle);
```

```
    }

    for handle in handles {
        handle.join().unwrap();
    }

    println!("Final vector: {:?}", *data.lock().unwrap());
}
```

The borrow checker ensures that the shared vector is accessed safely, even across multiple threads. The use of `Arc` and `Mutex` ensures proper synchronization.

Functional Programming and Borrow Checker

Rust's functional programming features can be combined with borrowing to create elegant and efficient code. Closures and iterators often rely on borrowing to avoid unnecessary data duplication.

Example: Borrowing in Iterators

```
fn main() {
    let numbers = vec![1, 2, 3, 4, 5];

    let squared: Vec<i32> = numbers.iter().map(|&x| x * x).collect();

    println!("Original: {:?}", numbers);
    println!("Squared: {:?}", squared);
}
```

The iterator borrows the vector `numbers`, ensuring that the original data remains intact while processing it.

Borrow Checker as a Design Tool

The borrow checker can inspire better program design by encouraging immutability and controlled mutability. Consider these design principles:

1. **Minimize Mutable State**: Limit the use of mutable references to specific scopes or encapsulate them within types like `Mutex` or `RefCell`.
2. **Encourage Immutability**: Use immutable references wherever possible to reduce complexity and improve safety.
3. **Use Lifetimes for Clarity**: Explicit lifetimes help communicate the relationship between different parts of your code.

Example: A State Machine

```rust
enum State<'a> {
    Start,
    Running(&'a str),
    Finished,
}

struct Machine<'a> {
    state: State<'a>,
}

impl<'a> Machine<'a> {
    fn new() -> Self {
        Machine { state: State::Start }
    }

    fn run(&mut self, input: &'a str) {
        self.state = State::Running(input);
    }

    fn finish(&mut self) {
        self.state = State::Finished;
    }

    fn display(&self) {
        match &self.state {
            State::Start => println!("Machine is in Start state."),
            State::Running(input) => println!("Machine is Running
with input: {}", input),
            State::Finished => println!("Machine has Finished."),
        }
    }
}

fn main() {
    let input = "Process data";
    let mut machine = Machine::new();
    machine.display();

    machine.run(input);
    machine.display();
```

```
    machine.finish();
    machine.display();
}
```

The state machine example uses lifetimes and borrowing to model transitions safely and predictably.

Summary

The borrow checker is more than a gatekeeper; it is a design tool that promotes safety, efficiency, and clarity. By embracing its rules, you can write code that is not only free from memory errors but also expressive and robust. Leveraging the borrow checker for better design requires a mindset shift from seeing it as an obstacle to recognizing its role as an ally in building high-quality software.

Chapter 6: Advanced Rust Features

Traits and Generics

Rust's traits and generics are powerful tools that allow for abstraction and code reuse without sacrificing performance. These features are central to Rust's design, enabling developers to write flexible, high-performance programs while maintaining strong type safety. This section delves into how traits and generics work and demonstrates their practical applications.

Understanding Traits

A **trait** in Rust is a collection of methods that define shared behavior. Traits are similar to interfaces in other languages like Java or C#, but they are more versatile and deeply integrated into Rust's type system.

Here's an example of defining and using a trait:

```rust
// Define a trait
trait Drawable {
    fn draw(&self);
}

// Implement the trait for a struct
struct Circle {
    radius: f64,
}

impl Drawable for Circle {
    fn draw(&self) {
        println!("Drawing a circle with radius {}", self.radius);
    }
}

struct Square {
    side: f64,
}

impl Drawable for Square {
    fn draw(&self) {
        println!("Drawing a square with side {}", self.side);
    }
}
```

```
// A function that uses the trait
fn render(object: &impl Drawable) {
    object.draw();
}

fn main() {
    let circle = Circle { radius: 5.0 };
    let square = Square { side: 3.0 };

    render(&circle);
    render(&square);
}
```

In this example:

1. The Drawable trait defines a single method, draw.
2. The Circle and Square structs implement the Drawable trait.
3. The render function accepts any object that implements the Drawable trait, demonstrating how traits enable polymorphism.

Generics in Rust

Generics allow you to write code that can operate on different types while ensuring type safety. They are particularly useful for creating reusable data structures and algorithms.

Generic Functions

Here's an example of a generic function:

```
fn largest<T: PartialOrd>(list: &[T]) -> &T {
    let mut largest = &list[0];
    for item in list {
        if item > largest {
            largest = item;
        }
    }
    largest
}

fn main() {
    let numbers = vec![34, 50, 25, 100, 65];
```

```
    let chars = vec!['a', 'x', 'm', 'q'];

    println!("The largest number is {}", largest(&numbers));
    println!("The largest char is {}", largest(&chars));
}
```

This function works with any type T that implements the PartialOrd trait, allowing comparisons.

Generic Structs

Structs can also be generic:

```
struct Point<T> {
    x: T,
    y: T,
}

fn main() {
    let integer_point = Point { x: 5, y: 10 };
    let float_point = Point { x: 1.0, y: 4.0 };

    println!("Integer    Point:    ({},    {})",    integer_point.x,
integer_point.y);
    println!("Float Point: ({}, {})", float_point.x, float_point.y);
}
```

This Point struct works for any type T, whether integers, floating-point numbers, or even custom types.

Generic Enums

Enums can also be generic, which is heavily used in Rust's standard library, such as the Option and Result enums:

```
enum Option<T> {
    Some(T),
    None,
}

enum Result<T, E> {
```

```
    Ok(T),
    Err(E),
}
```

These enums demonstrate how generics make Rust's error handling and optional values flexible and powerful.

Combining Traits and Generics

You can combine traits and generics to create even more flexible code. For example:

```
fn print_area<T: Drawable + Area>(shape: &T) {
    shape.draw();
    println!("Area: {}", shape.area());
}

trait Area {
    fn area(&self) -> f64;
}

impl Area for Circle {
    fn area(&self) -> f64 {
        3.14 * self.radius * self.radius
    }
}

impl Area for Square {
    fn area(&self) -> f64 {
        self.side * self.side
    }
}

fn main() {
    let circle = Circle { radius: 5.0 };
    let square = Square { side: 4.0 };

    print_area(&circle);
    print_area(&square);
}
```

This example demonstrates:

1. How multiple traits (`Drawable` and `Area`) can be combined.
2. How generics allow for abstract and reusable functions.

Lifetimes with Generics

Lifetimes are an essential part of Rust's generics system, ensuring memory safety when working with references. Here's a brief example:

```rust
fn longest<'a>(x: &'a str, y: &'a str) -> &'a str {
    if x.len() > y.len() {
        x
    } else {
        y
    }
}

fn main() {
    let string1 = String::from("hello");
    let string2 = String::from("world");

    let result = longest(&string1, &string2);
    println!("The longest string is {}", result);
}
```

In this example, the `'a` lifetime ensures that the returned reference is valid as long as both input references are valid.

Advanced Usage of Traits and Generics

Associated Types

Associated types simplify trait definitions by associating a type with a trait:

```rust
trait Iterator {
    type Item;
    fn next(&mut self) -> Option<Self::Item>;
}
```

This is used extensively in the standard library to define iterators.

Default Trait Implementations

Traits can have default method implementations:

```rust
trait Greet {
    fn greet(&self) {
        println!("Hello, World!");
    }
}

struct Person;

impl Greet for Person {}

fn main() {
    let person = Person;
    person.greet(); // Uses the default implementation
}
```

Blanket Implementations

Rust allows for blanket implementations, providing a trait implementation for all types that satisfy certain conditions:

```rust
impl<T: Display> ToString for T {
    fn to_string(&self) -> String {
        format!("{}", self)
    }
}
```

This is why any type implementing `Display` automatically has a `to_string` method.

Conclusion

Traits and generics are foundational to writing clean, efficient, and reusable Rust code. They enable powerful abstractions without compromising performance. By mastering these concepts, you can build complex systems with ease while maintaining Rust's guarantees of safety and correctness.

Macros: Writing DRY and Reusable Code

Macros in Rust are a powerful metaprogramming feature that enables developers to write DRY (Don't Repeat Yourself) and highly reusable code. Unlike functions, macros operate at compile time, allowing you to generate and manipulate code before it is compiled. This section explores Rust's macro system in depth, covering declarative macros, procedural macros, and their practical use cases.

Introduction to Macros

Macros in Rust come in three primary forms:

1. **Declarative Macros (macro_rules!)**: These macros are used for pattern matching and transforming input syntax.
2. **Procedural Macros**: These are custom macros defined in Rust libraries for tasks like attribute and function-like code generation.
3. **Derive Macros**: A subset of procedural macros, used to auto-generate code for traits.

Macros differ from functions in that they work with code structure rather than runtime values. This allows for powerful transformations that cannot be achieved with functions alone.

Declarative Macros with `macro_rules!`

Declarative macros use the `macro_rules!` syntax to match patterns and expand them into code. Here's a simple example of a macro to print debug information:

```
macro_rules! debug {
    ($val:expr) => {
        println!("{} = {:?}", stringify!($val), $val);
    };
}

fn main() {
    let x = 42;
    debug!(x);
}
```

This macro:

- Uses `stringify!` to convert the expression into a string.
- Prints both the variable name and its value.

Matching Multiple Patterns

Macros can match multiple patterns to provide flexibility:

```
macro_rules! calculate {
    (add $a:expr, $b:expr) => {
```

```rust
        $a + $b
    };
    (subtract $a:expr, $b:expr) => {
        $a - $b
    };
}

fn main() {
    let sum = calculate!(add 5, 3);
    let difference = calculate!(subtract 8, 2);

    println!("Sum: {}", sum);
    println!("Difference: {}", difference);
}
```

This macro can handle different operations based on the input pattern.

Repetition in Macros

Macros are excellent for handling repetitive code using the repetition syntax $(...)* or $(...)+. For example:

```rust
macro_rules! vec_of_strings {
    ($($x:expr),*) => {
        vec![$($x.to_string()),*]
    };
}

fn main() {
    let strings = vec_of_strings!["hello", "world", "rust"];
    println!("{:?}", strings);
}
```

This macro takes multiple expressions and converts them into a vector of strings.

Procedural Macros

Procedural macros provide even more power by allowing you to write code that generates code programmatically. They are defined in libraries and can process attributes, derive traits, or act as custom function-like macros.

Creating a Procedural Macro

To create a procedural macro, you start by creating a new library crate with the `proc-macro` feature enabled:

```
cargo new my_macro_lib --lib
cd my_macro_lib
```

Add the following to `Cargo.toml`:

```
[lib]
proc-macro = true
```

Define a procedural macro in `lib.rs`:

```
extern crate proc_macro;
use proc_macro::TokenStream;

#[proc_macro]
pub fn say_hello(_input: TokenStream) -> TokenStream {
    "fn hello() { println!(\"Hello, world!\"); }".parse().unwrap()
}
```

You can use this macro in another crate:

```
use my_macro_lib::say_hello;

say_hello!();

fn main() {
    hello();
}
```

Attribute Macros

Attribute macros are used to modify existing code, such as struct definitions:

```
use proc_macro::TokenStream;
```

```rust
#[proc_macro_attribute]
pub fn add_hello(_attr: TokenStream, item: TokenStream) -> TokenStream
{
    let input = item.to_string();
    let output = format!("{}\nfn hello() {{ println!(\"Hello!\"); }}",
input);
    output.parse().unwrap()
}
```

Apply this macro to a function:

```rust
#[add_hello]
fn greet() {
    println!("Greetings!");
}

fn main() {
    greet();
    hello();
}
```

Derive Macros

Derive macros automate the implementation of traits for custom types. For example, you can create a macro to implement a custom trait:

```rust
use proc_macro::TokenStream;

#[proc_macro_derive(MyTrait)]
pub fn my_trait_derive(_input: TokenStream) -> TokenStream {
    "impl MyTrait for MyStruct {
        fn my_function() {
            println!(\"Trait function called\");
        }
    }"
    .parse()
    .unwrap()
}
```

Practical Applications of Macros

Code Simplification

Macros can simplify complex, repetitive code. For instance, a macro can generate boilerplate code for initializing structs:

```
macro_rules! create_struct {
    ($name:ident, $($field:ident: $type:ty),*) => {
        struct $name {
            $($field: $type),*
        }
    };
}

create_struct!(Point, x: i32, y: i32);

fn main() {
    let point = Point { x: 10, y: 20 };
    println!("Point: ({}, {})", point.x, point.y);
}
```

Logging and Debugging

Macros can make logging more concise:

```
macro_rules! log {
    ($level:expr, $msg:expr) => {
        println!("[{}] {}", $level, $msg);
    };
}

fn main() {
    log!("INFO", "Application started");
    log!("ERROR", "An error occurred");
}
```

Creating Domain-Specific Languages (DSLs)

Macros are well-suited for creating DSLs. For example, a query builder:

```rust
macro_rules! query {
    ($table:ident, $($field:ident = $value:expr),*) => {
        format!(
            "SELECT * FROM {} WHERE {}",
            stringify!($table),
            vec![$(format!("{}    =    '{}'",    stringify!($field),
$value)),*].join(" AND ")
        )
    };
}

fn main() {
    let sql = query!(users, id = 1, name = "Alice");
    println!("{}", sql);
}
```

Best Practices for Writing Macros

1. **Minimize Complexity**: Use macros sparingly to avoid making the codebase harder to understand.
2. **Document Your Macros**: Include comprehensive documentation to clarify the macro's behavior.
3. **Combine Macros with Traits and Functions**: Use macros to generate code that integrates well with Rust's type system.

Conclusion

Macros are a cornerstone of Rust's metaprogramming capabilities, offering unmatched flexibility and efficiency. Whether you're simplifying repetitive patterns, generating boilerplate code, or creating DSLs, macros enable you to push the boundaries of what your Rust programs can do. By understanding declarative and procedural macros, you can unlock powerful techniques to make your codebase more robust and expressive.

Concurrency and Parallelism in Rust

Concurrency and parallelism are essential for building high-performance applications that make efficient use of modern multicore processors. Rust's unique ownership model and its strong emphasis on safety make it particularly well-suited for handling concurrent and parallel programming without common pitfalls like data races and memory corruption. This section explores the tools and techniques available in Rust for writing concurrent and parallel code, including threads, async programming, and parallel processing libraries.

Threads in Rust

Rust provides a powerful standard library for working with threads. Threads allow you to perform tasks concurrently, enabling multiple operations to happen simultaneously.

Creating Threads

Creating threads in Rust is straightforward with the `std::thread` module:

```rust
use std::thread;

fn main() {
    let handle = thread::spawn(|| {
        for i in 1..5 {
            println!("Hello from spawned thread: {}", i);
        }
    });

    for i in 1..5 {
        println!("Hello from main thread: {}", i);
    }

    handle.join().unwrap();
}
```

In this example:

- `thread::spawn` starts a new thread.
- `handle.join()` ensures the spawned thread completes before the program exits.

Sharing Data Between Threads

To share data between threads, Rust provides thread-safe abstractions like `Arc` and `Mutex`.

```rust
use std::sync::{Arc, Mutex};
use std::thread;

fn main() {
    let counter = Arc::new(Mutex::new(0));
    let mut handles = vec![];

    for _ in 0..10 {
        let counter = Arc::clone(&counter);
        let handle = thread::spawn(move || {
```

```
            let mut num = counter.lock().unwrap();
            *num += 1;
        });
        handles.push(handle);
    }

    for handle in handles {
        handle.join().unwrap();
    }

    println!("Final counter value: {}", *counter.lock().unwrap());
}
```

In this code:

- Arc (Atomic Reference Counted) ensures safe shared ownership of the Mutex.
- Mutex provides mutual exclusion, ensuring only one thread can access the data at a time.

Handling Thread Panics

Threads in Rust can panic without crashing the main thread. Use Result to handle panics gracefully:

```
use std::thread;

fn main() {
    let handle = thread::spawn(|| {
        panic!("Something went wrong!");
    });

    match handle.join() {
        Ok(_) => println!("Thread completed successfully."),
        Err(err) => println!("Thread panicked: {:?}", err),
    }
}
```

Async Programming

Rust's async/await syntax simplifies asynchronous programming, enabling efficient I/O-bound tasks without blocking threads. Asynchronous programming is based on the concept of tasks that can pause and resume.

Writing Asynchronous Functions

Define asynchronous functions using the `async` keyword:

```rust
async fn fetch_data() -> String {
    "Data fetched asynchronously".to_string()
}

#[tokio::main]
async fn main() {
    let result = fetch_data().await;
    println!("{}", result);
}
```

Here:

- `async fn` defines an asynchronous function.
- `.await` pauses the function until the asynchronous task completes.

Using Async Libraries

The `tokio` and `async-std` libraries provide runtime support for asynchronous programming:

```rust
use tokio::time::{sleep, Duration};

#[tokio::main]
async fn main() {
    let task1 = async {
        sleep(Duration::from_secs(2)).await;
        println!("Task 1 completed");
    };

    let task2 = async {
        sleep(Duration::from_secs(1)).await;
        println!("Task 2 completed");
    };

    tokio::join!(task1, task2);
}
```

This code demonstrates:

- Running multiple tasks concurrently using `tokio::join!`.
- Non-blocking delays with `sleep`.

Channels for Async Communication

Channels provide a way to communicate between tasks. Use `tokio::sync::mpsc` for asynchronous channels:

```
use tokio::sync::mpsc;

#[tokio::main]
async fn main() {
    let (tx, mut rx) = mpsc::channel(32);

    tokio::spawn(async move {
        tx.send("Hello from async task").await.unwrap();
    });

    while let Some(msg) = rx.recv().await {
        println!("Received: {}", msg);
    }
}
```

Parallelism with Rayon's Data Parallelism

Rust's `rayon` library is ideal for parallel processing. It provides high-level abstractions for dividing work across threads.

Parallel Iterators

Parallel iterators distribute iterations across multiple threads:

```
use rayon::prelude::*;

fn main() {
    let numbers: Vec<i32> = (1..10).collect();
    let sum: i32 = numbers.par_iter().sum();
    println!("Sum of numbers: {}", sum);
}
```

In this example:

- `par_iter` enables parallel iteration.
- The `sum` operation is distributed across threads.

Parallelizing Complex Workloads

Rayon simplifies complex workloads, such as matrix multiplication:

```rust
use rayon::prelude::*;

fn main() {
    let matrix_a = vec![vec![1, 2], vec![3, 4]];
    let matrix_b = vec![vec![5, 6], vec![7, 8]];

    let result: Vec<Vec<i32>> = matrix_a
        .par_iter()
        .map(|row| {
            matrix_b[0]
                .iter()
                .zip(&matrix_b[1])
                .map(|(a, b)| row[0] * a + row[1] * b)
                .collect()
        })
        .collect();

    println!("{:?}", result);
}
```

This demonstrates:

- Mapping operations across rows in parallel.
- Combining results efficiently.

Comparing Concurrency and Parallelism

Concurrency and parallelism address different aspects of multitasking:

- **Concurrency** is about managing multiple tasks at the same time, often involving I/O-bound workloads.
- **Parallelism** focuses on dividing a single task into smaller pieces for simultaneous execution, ideal for CPU-bound tasks.

Best Practices for Concurrency and Parallelism

1. **Minimize Shared State**: Avoid unnecessary shared data to reduce complexity.

2. **Leverage Libraries**: Use established libraries like `tokio` for concurrency and `rayon` for parallelism.
3. **Understand the Workload**: Choose concurrency for I/O-bound tasks and parallelism for CPU-bound tasks.
4. **Test Thoroughly**: Concurrent and parallel programs can be challenging to debug. Test for edge cases.

Conclusion

Rust's approach to concurrency and parallelism is both powerful and safe. By leveraging threads, async/await, and libraries like `rayon`, developers can build high-performance applications that fully utilize modern hardware while avoiding common pitfalls. Mastering these tools will unlock the potential of writing efficient, scalable, and robust software in Rust.

Chapter 7: Working with Rust Ecosystem Tools

Cargo: Package Management and Build System

Cargo is the Rust package manager and build system, a cornerstone of the Rust programming experience. Whether you are a beginner or an experienced developer, mastering Cargo is essential for managing dependencies, building projects, running tests, and streamlining development workflows. This section explores Cargo's features in detail, offering a comprehensive guide to its functionality.

What is Cargo?

Cargo is Rust's default package manager, designed to simplify the process of managing project dependencies and build processes. It also serves as a tool for creating, building, and distributing Rust packages, commonly referred to as "crates." Cargo ensures that your development process remains seamless, efficient, and aligned with Rust's philosophy of safety and performance.

Initializing a New Project

Creating a new Rust project with Cargo is straightforward. Use the following command to create a new binary project:

```
cargo new my_project
```

This command creates a directory named `my_project` containing the following structure:

```
my_project/
├── Cargo.toml
└── src/
    └── main.rs
```

- **Cargo.toml**: The manifest file where you define dependencies, project metadata, and configuration.
- **src/main.rs**: The entry point for your application.

To create a library project instead, use:

```
cargo new my_library --lib
```

Building and Running Projects

Cargo handles the build process automatically. Run the following command to compile your project:

```
cargo build
```

This generates an optimized binary in the `target/debug/` directory. To execute the program directly, use:

```
cargo run
```

For production-ready builds, Cargo offers the `--release` flag:

```
cargo build --release
```

This generates an optimized binary in the `target/release/` directory, suitable for deployment.

Managing Dependencies

Dependencies in Rust are managed via the `Cargo.toml` file. To add a dependency, specify it under the `[dependencies]` section:

```
[dependencies]

serde = "1.0"
```

Run the following command to download and integrate the specified dependency:

```
cargo build
```

Cargo fetches the dependency from Crates.io and ensures compatibility with your project.

Version Constraints

Rust supports semantic versioning. Examples of version constraints include:

- `serde = "1.0"`: Matches any $1.0.x$ version.
- `serde = "1.0.0"`: Matches exactly version $1.0.0$.
- `serde = ">=1.0, <2.0"`: Matches versions $1.x.x$.

Cargo Commands Overview

Here are some of the most commonly used Cargo commands:

Command	Description
`cargo build`	Compiles the project.
`cargo run`	Builds and runs the project.
`cargo test`	Runs tests defined in the project.
`cargo clean`	Removes compiled artifacts.
`cargo doc`	Generates documentation for the project.

`cargo check`	Checks for errors without building artifacts.
`cargo update`	Updates dependencies to the latest versions.

Creating and Publishing Crates

Cargo simplifies the process of sharing your Rust packages. To create a crate:

Prepare your project and ensure the metadata in `Cargo.toml` is accurate: toml

```toml
[package]

name = "my_crate"

version = "0.1.0"

authors = ["Your Name <your.email@example.com>"]

description = "A sample Rust crate"

license = "MIT"

repository = "https://github.com/username/my_crate"
```

1.

Log   in   to   Crates.io:
bash

```bash
cargo login
```

2.

Publish   your   crate:
bash

```bash
cargo publish
```

3.

Your crate is now available for others to use via Crates.io.

Using Workspaces

Cargo workspaces allow you to manage multiple related projects in a single repository. A workspace is defined in a `Cargo.toml` file at the root of the repository:

```
[workspace]
members = [
    "project1",
    "project2",
]
```

Each member can have its own `Cargo.toml` file and dependencies but shares a common `target/` directory for build artifacts.

Managing Profiles

Cargo provides two build profiles: `dev` and `release`. These profiles can be customized in `Cargo.toml`:

```
[profile.dev]
opt-level = 0


[profile.release]
opt-level = 3
```

The `opt-level` determines the level of optimization applied during compilation. Higher levels result in faster binaries at the cost of longer compile times.

Testing with Cargo

Cargo integrates seamlessly with Rust's testing framework. Define tests in your project using the `#[test]` attribute:

```
#[cfg(test)]

mod tests {

    #[test]

    fn test_example() {

        assert_eq!(2 + 2, 4);

    }

}
```

Run tests with:

```
cargo test
```

Building Documentation

Cargo can generate HTML documentation for your project and its dependencies:

```
cargo doc --open
```

This command creates a `target/doc/` directory and opens the documentation in your default web browser.

Conclusion

Cargo is an indispensable tool in the Rust ecosystem, streamlining every aspect of development. By mastering Cargo, you can efficiently manage dependencies, build projects, run tests, and create production-ready applications. Its versatility and ease of use are vital for any Rust developer.

Crates.io and the Rust Community

Crates.io is the official package registry for Rust, hosting a vast collection of open-source crates that developers can integrate into their projects. This section delves into how to use Crates.io effectively, explores best practices for managing dependencies, and highlights the vibrant Rust community that supports and enhances the ecosystem.

What is Crates.io?

Crates.io is the central repository where developers publish and share Rust libraries (crates). It serves as a one-stop shop for finding high-quality libraries that extend Rust's functionality. Crates.io also integrates seamlessly with Cargo, making it easy to add and manage dependencies in your projects.

Key features of Crates.io:

- **Searchable Registry**: Easily find crates based on keywords, categories, and popularity.
- **Semantic Versioning**: Ensures compatibility between your project and its dependencies.
- **Community Contributions**: Leverages the collective effort of Rust developers worldwide.

Searching for Crates

To find a crate, visit Crates.io and use the search functionality. You can search by:

- **Name**: If you know the crate's name, simply enter it into the search bar.
- **Keywords**: Use relevant terms to discover crates related to specific functionality.
- **Categories**: Browse crates organized by domains like "web development" or "data science."

For example, to find a crate for JSON serialization, search for "JSON" or "serialization."

Adding Crates to Your Project

Once you identify a suitable crate, adding it to your project is straightforward. Open your `Cargo.toml` file and add the crate under the `[dependencies]` section. For instance, to add the popular `serde` crate:

```
[dependencies]

serde = "1.0"
```

Run the following command to download and integrate the dependency:

```
cargo build
```

Cargo resolves the dependency, fetches it from Crates.io, and ensures it is compatible with your project.

Managing Dependency Features

Many crates on Crates.io provide optional features that enable additional functionality. You can specify which features to include in your `Cargo.toml` file. For example, to use `serde` with its `derive` feature:

```
[dependencies]

serde = { version = "1.0", features = ["derive"] }
```

Optional features allow you to tailor dependencies to your project's needs without unnecessary bloat.

Exploring Popular Crates

Crates.io offers a wealth of popular libraries that cover diverse use cases. Here are some commonly used crates:

- **Tokio**: Asynchronous programming and event-driven applications.
- **Serde**: Serialization and deserialization of data formats.
- **Actix-web**: Building web applications and APIs.
- **Clap**: Command-line argument parsing.
- **Rand**: Random number generation.

To add any of these crates, follow the same process of modifying your `Cargo.toml` file and running `cargo build`.

Publishing Your Own Crates

Crates.io is not just for consuming libraries but also for sharing your work with the community. Publishing a crate involves the following steps:

Step 1: Prepare Your Crate

Ensure your project meets the publishing requirements:

- **Unique Name**: The crate name must be unique on Crates.io.

Valid Metadata: Update your `Cargo.toml` file with accurate metadata: toml

```toml
[package]

name = "my_crate"

version = "0.1.0"

authors = ["Your Name <your.email@example.com>"]

description = "A sample crate for demonstration purposes"

license = "MIT"

repository = "https://github.com/username/my_crate"
```

-

Step 2: Test and Verify

Thoroughly test your crate to ensure it functions as expected. You can use the following commands:

- `cargo test`: Runs all defined tests.
- `cargo check`: Checks for errors without building the project.

Step 3: Login to Crates.io

Authenticate with Crates.io using Cargo:

```
cargo login
```

This command prompts you to enter an API token available from your Crates.io account settings.

Step 4: Publish the Crate

Publish your crate with the following command:

```
cargo publish
```

Cargo packages your crate, uploads it to Crates.io, and makes it available for others to use.

Best Practices for Publishing Crates

To ensure your crate stands out and benefits the community, follow these best practices:

- **Comprehensive Documentation**: Include clear examples and explanations in your crate's README file and Rust doc comments.
- **Semantic Versioning**: Follow semantic versioning principles to communicate changes effectively.
- **License Your Code**: Use a permissive license like MIT or Apache-2.0 to encourage adoption.
- **Respond to Feedback**: Actively engage with users of your crate, addressing issues and accepting contributions.

Engaging with the Rust Community

The Rust community is one of the most active and welcoming in the programming world. Here's how you can get involved:

Participate in Forums

The Rust Users Forum is an excellent place to ask questions, share knowledge, and engage with other developers. Whether you're a beginner or an expert, the community is eager to help.

Join the Rust Discord

The Rust Discord is a vibrant space for real-time discussions. It includes channels for specific topics, such as async programming, web development, and embedded systems.

Contribute to Open Source

Many Rust projects on GitHub welcome contributions. Look for issues labeled "good first issue" to get started. By contributing, you not only improve your skills but also give back to the community.

Attend Conferences and Meetups

Rust conferences like RustConf and local meetups provide opportunities to learn, network, and share your experiences with others. Check the Rust Community Calendar for upcoming events.

Conclusion

Crates.io and the Rust community form the backbone of the Rust ecosystem. By leveraging the resources available on Crates.io and actively participating in the community, you can enhance your projects, learn from others, and contribute to the growth of Rust. Whether you are consuming libraries, publishing your own crates, or engaging with fellow developers, the possibilities are endless.

Debugging and Testing in Rust

Debugging and testing are crucial aspects of software development, ensuring that code behaves as expected and meets quality standards. Rust provides robust tools and frameworks to facilitate these processes, enabling developers to build reliable and performant applications. This section explores debugging techniques, testing methodologies, and best practices for debugging and testing Rust programs.

Debugging in Rust

Debugging in Rust involves identifying and resolving issues in code. Rust's strong type system and ownership model catch many bugs at compile time, but runtime errors can still occur. Tools like `println!`, logging libraries, and integrated development environments (IDEs) can assist in diagnosing and fixing issues.

Using `println!` for Debugging

The simplest way to debug Rust code is to use the `println!` macro to print variables and messages:

```rust
fn main() {

    let x = 10;

    println!("The value of x is: {}", x);

    let y = x + 5;

    println!("The value of y is: {}", y);

}
```

While `println!` is useful for small projects or quick debugging, it is not suitable for larger, complex applications. For more advanced debugging, use tools like the Rust debugger.

Debugging with `debug!` and `trace!`

The `log` crate provides structured logging with levels like `debug!`, `info!`, `warn!`, and `error!`. This method is more robust than `println!`:

Add the `log` and `env_logger` crates to your `Cargo.toml` file: toml

```toml
[dependencies]
```

```
log = "0.4"

env_logger = "0.10"
```

1.

Initialize   the   logger   in   your   main   function:
rust

```
use log::{debug, info};


fn main() {

    env_logger::init();

    let x = 10;

    debug!("Debugging value: x = {}", x);

    info!("Application started successfully");

}
```

2.

Run your program with the RUST_LOG environment variable set to the desired log level:
bash

```
RUST_LOG=debug cargo run
```

3.

This approach enables selective logging and integrates well with larger systems.

Debugging with GDB and LLDB

For more advanced debugging, use GDB or LLDB, popular debuggers that support Rust. Compile your program with debugging symbols by using the --debug flag (default in development mode):

```
cargo build
```

Then, run the debugger:

For   GDB:
bash

```
gdb target/debug/your_program
```

-

For   LLDB:
bash

```
lldb target/debug/your_program
```

-

These tools allow you to set breakpoints, inspect variables, and step through code.

Using IDEs for Debugging

Integrated development environments like Visual Studio Code (with the Rust Analyzer extension) and IntelliJ IDEA (with the IntelliJ Rust plugin) provide debugging capabilities. They allow you to set breakpoints, view call stacks, and inspect variables in a graphical interface.

Writing and Running Tests

Testing in Rust ensures that your code behaves as intended and prevents regressions. Rust's built-in test framework simplifies the creation and execution of tests.

Unit Tests

Unit tests validate individual components in isolation. Define unit tests within the same file as the code under test, using the #[cfg(test)] and #[test] attributes:

```
#[cfg(test)]

mod tests {

    #[test]

    fn test_addition() {

        let result = 2 + 2;

        assert_eq!(result, 4);

    }
```

```
    #[test]

    fn test_subtraction() {

        let result = 5 - 3;

        assert_eq!(result, 2);

    }

}
```

Run tests with:

```
cargo test
```

This command executes all tests and reports the results.

Integration Tests

Integration tests validate the behavior of multiple components working together. Place integration tests in the tests directory of your project:

```
my_project/

├── src/

│   └── lib.rs

└── tests/

    ├── test_one.rs

    └── test_two.rs
```

For example, in tests/test_one.rs:

```
use my_project::add;


#[test]

fn test_add_function() {

    let result = add(2, 3);

    assert_eq!(result, 5);

}
```

Run all integration tests with:

```
cargo test
```

Testing Error Cases

Rust's Result type is useful for testing error cases. Use the #[should_panic] attribute to test scenarios where your code should panic:

```
#[cfg(test)]

mod tests {

    #[test]

    #[should_panic]

    fn test_divide_by_zero() {

        let _ = 10 / 0;

    }

}
```

Alternatively, test custom error handling with `Result`:

```rust
fn divide(a: i32, b: i32) -> Result<i32, String> {

    if b == 0 {

        Err("Cannot divide by zero".to_string())

    } else {

        Ok(a / b)

    }

}


#[cfg(test)]

mod tests {

    use super::*;

    #[test]

    fn test_divide_success() {

        assert_eq!(divide(10, 2), Ok(5));

    }


    #[test]

    fn test_divide_error() {

        assert_eq!(divide(10,    0),    Err("Cannot    divide    by
zero".to_string()));

    }

}
```

Code Coverage

To measure test coverage, use tools like `cargo-tarpaulin`:

Install `cargo-tarpaulin`:
bash

```
cargo install cargo-tarpaulin
```

1.

Run the coverage analysis:
bash

```
cargo tarpaulin
```

2.

This generates a report showing which lines of code were executed during testing.

Best Practices for Debugging and Testing

1. **Write Tests Early**: Adopt a test-driven development (TDD) approach to catch bugs early.
2. **Use Mocking**: Mock external dependencies for isolated testing.
3. **Focus on Edge Cases**: Test boundary conditions, invalid inputs, and error scenarios.
4. **Automate Testing**: Use CI/CD pipelines to automate test execution on every commit.
5. **Refactor with Confidence**: Write comprehensive tests to enable safe refactoring.

Conclusion

Debugging and testing are integral to building robust Rust applications. Rust's tools, from `println!` to advanced testing frameworks, empower developers to identify issues and ensure code quality. By following the methodologies and best practices outlined here, you can streamline your development process and deliver reliable software.

Chapter 8: Practical Applications

Systems Programming with Rust

Rust's focus on safety, performance, and concurrency makes it an excellent choice for systems programming. From operating system kernels to network protocols, Rust has the capability to handle low-level programming tasks while providing a high degree of reliability. This section explores how to use Rust effectively in systems programming by examining core principles, common practices, and practical examples.

Why Use Rust for Systems Programming?

Rust bridges the gap between low-level programming languages like C and high-level languages such as Python. Here's why Rust stands out in systems programming:

- **Memory Safety**: Rust's ownership model prevents common memory errors such as null pointer dereferencing, buffer overflows, and data races.
- **Performance**: Rust compiles directly to machine code, allowing it to perform on par with C and C++.
- **Concurrency**: Rust's safe concurrency model ensures data race-free code at compile time, making it ideal for modern, multi-core processors.
- **Expressiveness**: With modern language features like pattern matching, traits, and generics, Rust combines safety with expressiveness.

Key Concepts in Systems Programming with Rust

1. Memory Management

Rust eliminates the need for manual memory management by enforcing ownership and borrowing rules. This prevents common issues like double frees and memory leaks while allowing deterministic resource cleanup through the Drop trait.

Example of ownership in practice:

```
fn main() {

    let data = String::from("Hello, Rust!");

    process_data(data);

    // println!("{}", data); // Uncommenting this will cause a
compile-time error

}
```

```rust
fn process_data(data: String) {

    println!("{}", data);

}
```

In the above example, the ownership of `data` is moved to the `process_data` function, preventing unintended access after the move.

2. Low-Level Access

Rust provides low-level access comparable to C, including pointer manipulation via `unsafe` blocks when required. However, such usage is limited to specific scenarios to maintain safety guarantees.

```rust
fn unsafe_example() {

    let x: i32 = 42;

    let r: *const i32 = &x;


    unsafe {

        println!("Value at r: {}", *r);

    }

}
```

3. Concurrency and Multithreading

Rust's standard library includes primitives for thread management and synchronization, such as `std::thread`, `Mutex`, and `RwLock`. These tools ensure that shared data access is safe and efficient.

```rust
use std::sync::{Arc, Mutex};
```

```rust
use std::thread;

fn main() {
    let data = Arc::new(Mutex::new(vec![1, 2, 3]));
    let mut handles = vec![];

    for i in 0..3 {
        let data = Arc::clone(&data);
        let handle = thread::spawn(move || {
            let mut data = data.lock().unwrap();
            data.push(i);
        });
        handles.push(handle);
    }

    for handle in handles {
        handle.join().unwrap();
    }

    println!("{:?}", *data.lock().unwrap());
}
```

The Arc ensures multiple threads can share ownership of the data, and the Mutex ensures safe, synchronized access.

Building a Simple File System Utility

To demonstrate Rust's capabilities in systems programming, let's build a simple file system utility to list files and directories with metadata.

Step 1: Setting Up

Create a new project using Cargo:

```
cargo new file_system_utility

cd file_system_utility
```

Add the walkdir crate to the Cargo.toml file for traversing directories:

```
[dependencies]

walkdir = "2.3.3"
```

Step 2: Implementing the Utility

Below is the main code for a file system utility:

```rust
use std::fs;

use std::io;

use std::path::Path;

use walkdir::WalkDir;


fn main() -> io::Result<()> {

    let path = ".";

    list_files_and_metadata(path)?;

    Ok(())

}
```

```rust
fn list_files_and_metadata<P: AsRef<Path>>(path: P) -> io::Result<()>
{
    for entry in WalkDir::new(path) {
        let entry = entry?;
        let metadata = fs::metadata(entry.path())?;
        println!(
            "File: {:?}, Size: {} bytes, Is Directory: {}",
            entry.path(),
            metadata.len(),
            metadata.is_dir()
        );
    }
    Ok(())
}
```

Step 3: Running the Program

Compile and run the program:

```
cargo run
```

This will recursively list all files and directories starting from the current directory, along with their size and type.

Interfacing with C Libraries

Rust's extern keyword allows you to call C functions. This is particularly useful for leveraging existing C libraries in systems programming.

Example: Calling a C Library

Here's an example using the `libc` crate to call a C function:

```rust
extern crate libc;

use libc::printf;
use std::ffi::CString;

fn main() {
    let c_string = CString::new("Hello from C!\n").unwrap();
    unsafe {
        printf(c_string.as_ptr());
    }
}
```

Add `libc` to your dependencies in `Cargo.toml`:

```toml
[dependencies]
libc = "0.2"
```

Debugging Systems Programs

Debugging low-level code is crucial in systems programming. Rust provides tools such as `println!` macros, the `log` crate, and integration with debuggers like GDB.

Using `log` for Structured Logging

```rust
use log::{info, warn};

use simple_logger::SimpleLogger;


fn main() {

    SimpleLogger::new().init().unwrap();


    info!("Application started");

    warn!("This is a warning message");

}
```

Add `log` and `simple_logger` to `Cargo.toml`:

```toml
[dependencies]

log = "0.4"

simple_logger = "4.0"
```

Conclusion

Rust's robust feature set makes it a powerful tool for systems programming. Its emphasis on safety and performance allows developers to write reliable and efficient low-level code. Whether building utilities, interfacing with other languages, or managing concurrency, Rust provides the tools and ecosystem support necessary for success. Systems programming with Rust is not just about managing memory or handling threads; it's about crafting elegant and maintainable solutions to complex problems.

Building Web Applications Using Actix and Rocket

Web development is a domain where Rust excels due to its performance, safety guarantees, and rich ecosystem. Frameworks like Actix and Rocket make building web applications in Rust intuitive and efficient. This section explores these frameworks, their features, and how to create functional web applications using them.

Why Rust for Web Development?

Rust offers several advantages for web development:

- **Performance**: Rust's compiled nature ensures that web applications are highly performant, comparable to applications written in C or C++.
- **Memory Safety**: Rust prevents common programming errors, making web applications robust and secure.
- **Concurrency**: Rust's ownership model ensures data race-free multithreading, enabling highly scalable web applications.
- **Modern Tooling**: Rust provides excellent tools like `cargo`, making dependency management and testing seamless.

Actix Web Framework

Actix is a powerful, actor-based framework for building asynchronous web applications in Rust. It is known for its performance and flexibility.

Setting Up an Actix Project

To get started, create a new project:

```
cargo new actix_web_app

cd actix_web_app
```

Add `actix-web` to the `Cargo.toml` file:

```
[dependencies]

actix-web = "4.0"
```

Creating a Simple Actix Web Application

Below is a basic Actix web server:

```
use actix_web::{web, App, HttpServer, Responder};
```

```
async fn index() -> impl Responder {

    "Welcome to Actix Web!"

}


#[actix_web::main]

async fn main() -> std::io::Result<()> {

    HttpServer::new(|| {

        App::new()

            .route("/", web::get().to(index))

    })

    .bind("127.0.0.1:8080")?

    .run()

    .await

}
```

- **Explanation**:
  - The index function handles HTTP GET requests to the root URL.
  - The HttpServer binds the application to 127.0.0.1:8080.
  - The App configures routes for the application.

Run the application:

```
cargo run
```

Visit http://127.0.0.1:8080 in your browser to see the response.

Handling JSON Data

Actix provides robust support for working with JSON. Below is an example of a route that accepts and returns JSON data:

```rust
use actix_web::{web, App, HttpServer, Responder};

use serde::{Deserialize, Serialize};


#[derive(Serialize, Deserialize)]

struct User {

    name: String,

    age: u8,

}


async fn create_user(user: web::Json<User>) -> impl Responder {

    format!("User {} created, age {}", user.name, user.age)

}


#[actix_web::main]

async fn main() -> std::io::Result<()> {

    HttpServer::new(|| {

        App::new()

            .route("/create_user", web::post().to(create_user))

    })

    .bind("127.0.0.1:8080")?

    .run()

    .await

}
```

- Add `serde` and `serde_json` to your dependencies for JSON handling:

```
[dependencies]

actix-web = "4.0"

serde = { version = "1.0", features = ["derive"] }

serde_json = "1.0"
```

Send a POST request with JSON data to `/create_user`:

```
{

    "name": "Alice",

    "age": 30

}
```

The server responds with `User Alice created, age 30.`

Rocket Web Framework

Rocket is another popular web framework in Rust, emphasizing ease of use and developer productivity. It uses Rust's type system to enforce safety and correctness.

Setting Up a Rocket Project

Create a new project:

```
cargo new rocket_web_app

cd rocket_web_app
```

Add Rocket to your `Cargo.toml` file:

```toml
[dependencies]
rocket = "0.5.0-rc.1"
```

Creating a Simple Rocket Application

Below is an example of a basic Rocket application:

```rust
#[macro_use] extern crate rocket;

#[get("/")]
fn index() -> &'static str {
    "Welcome to Rocket!"
}

#[launch]
fn rocket() -> _ {
    rocket::build().mount("/", routes![index])
}
```

Run the application with:

```
cargo run
```

Visit `http://127.0.0.1:8000` in your browser to see the response.

Handling JSON Data

Rocket makes it easy to handle JSON requests and responses. Below is an example:

```rust
use rocket::serde::{Deserialize, Serialize, json::Json};


#[derive(Serialize, Deserialize)]
struct User {
    name: String,
    age: u8,
}


#[post("/create_user", format = "json", data = "<user>")]
fn create_user(user: Json<User>) -> String {
    format!("User {} created, age {}", user.name, user.age)
}


#[launch]
fn rocket() -> _ {
    rocket::build().mount("/", routes![create_user])
}
```

Send a POST request with JSON data to /create_user:

```json
{
    "name": "Bob",
```

```
    "age": 25

}
```

The server responds with `User Bob created, age 25.`

Comparing Actix and Rocket

Feature	Actix	Rocket
Performance	High-performance, async-based	High-performance
Ease of Use	Moderate	Beginner-friendly
Asynchronous	Fully async	Async support (in newer versions)
Ecosystem	Large, with many middlewares	Smaller, tightly integrated

Conclusion

Both Actix and Rocket are excellent choices for building web applications in Rust. Actix shines in performance-critical applications, while Rocket offers a more user-friendly experience for developers new to Rust. The choice depends on your project requirements and familiarity with asynchronous programming. Rust's growing ecosystem ensures that web development with these frameworks will continue to evolve, offering more features and flexibility for developers.

Rust in Game Development and Embedded Systems

Rust has gained considerable traction in game development and embedded systems due to its focus on performance, safety, and control over system resources. This section explores how Rust can be used to create games and build software for embedded systems, highlighting key libraries, frameworks, and techniques.

Game Development with Rust

Game development involves working with graphics, physics, and sound while maintaining high performance. Rust's memory safety and concurrency features make it a strong choice for developing games that are fast, reliable, and scalable.

Why Use Rust for Game Development?

- **Performance**: Rust's zero-cost abstractions allow games to run efficiently without sacrificing safety.
- **Concurrency**: Rust's ownership model makes it easier to write multi-threaded code, which is critical for game engines.
- **Ecosystem**: Libraries like Bevy and Amethyst simplify game development by providing high-level abstractions.

Bevy: A Modern Game Engine

Bevy is a lightweight and modular game engine built with Rust. It uses an Entity-Component-System (ECS) architecture, which makes it easier to manage complex game logic.

Setting Up a Bevy Project

Create a new project:

```
cargo new bevy_game

cd bevy_game
```

Add Bevy to your `Cargo.toml` file:

```
[dependencies]

bevy = "0.11"
```

Creating a Simple Game with Bevy

Below is an example of a simple Bevy application that displays a moving square:

```
use bevy::prelude::*;
```

```rust
fn main() {

    App::new()

        .add_plugins(DefaultPlugins)

        .add_startup_system(setup)

        .add_system(move_square)

        .run();

}


fn     setup(mut     commands:     Commands,     mut     materials:
ResMut<Assets<ColorMaterial>>) {

    commands.spawn(Camera2dBundle::default());

    commands.spawn(SpriteBundle {

        material: materials.add(Color::rgb(0.5, 0.5, 1.0).into()),

        sprite: Sprite::new(Vec2::new(50.0, 50.0)),

        ..Default::default()

    });

}


fn move_square(mut query: Query<&mut Transform, With<Sprite>>, time:
Res<Time>) {

    for mut transform in query.iter_mut() {

        transform.translation.x += 100.0 * time.delta_seconds();

    }

}
```

- **Explanation**:
  - A 2D camera and a square sprite are set up in the `setup` system.
  - The `move_square` system moves the square along the x-axis, demonstrating simple game logic.

Run the application with:

```
cargo run
```

Adding Interactivity

You can add input handling to make the game interactive. Below is an example that moves the square based on keyboard input:

```rust
fn move_square(

    keyboard_input: Res<Input<KeyCode>>,

    mut query: Query<&mut Transform, With<Sprite>>,

) {

    for mut transform in query.iter_mut() {

        if keyboard_input.pressed(KeyCode::Left) {

            transform.translation.x -= 5.0;

        }

        if keyboard_input.pressed(KeyCode::Right) {

            transform.translation.x += 5.0;

        }

    }

}
```

Other Game Engines and Libraries

- **Amethyst**: A data-driven game engine for 2D and 3D games.
- **ggez**: A lightweight library for 2D game development, inspired by the Love2D engine.
- **macroquad**: A simple and fast library for building cross-platform games.

Embedded Systems with Rust

Embedded systems programming involves working directly with hardware, often in resource-constrained environments. Rust's safety guarantees and fine-grained control over hardware resources make it ideal for embedded development.

Why Use Rust for Embedded Systems?

- **No Runtime Overhead**: Rust does not rely on garbage collection or other runtime systems, making it suitable for constrained environments.
- **Safety**: Rust ensures memory safety and prevents undefined behavior, which is critical for embedded systems.
- **Concurrency**: Rust's safe multithreading capabilities are useful for embedded systems with multiple peripherals or tasks.

Getting Started with Rust for Embedded Systems

To work with embedded systems, you'll need the following:

Install the Nightly Toolchain: Rust's embedded development requires nightly features:
bash

```
rustup install nightly

rustup default nightly
```

1.

Add the Embedded Target: Install the target for your embedded system. For ARM Cortex-M, use:
bash

```
rustup target add thumbv7em-none-eabihf
```

2.

Set Up the Development Environment: Use a template project to bootstrap your setup. The `cortex-m-quickstart` template is a good starting point:
bash

```
cargo generate --git https://github.com/rust-embedded/cortex-m-quickstart
```

```
cd project_name
```

3.

Blinking an LED

The "Hello World" of embedded programming is blinking an LED. Below is an example for a microcontroller using the `stm32f4xx-hal` crate:

```rust
#![no_std]
#![no_main]

use cortex_m_rt::entry;
use stm32f4xx_hal::{pac, prelude::*};

#[entry]
fn main() -> ! {
    let dp = pac::Peripherals::take().unwrap();
    let gpioa = dp.GPIOA.split();
    let mut led = gpioa.pa5.into_push_pull_output();

    loop {
        led.set_high().unwrap();
        cortex_m::asm::delay(8_000_000);
        led.set_low().unwrap();
        cortex_m::asm::delay(8_000_000);
    }
}
```

- **Explanation**:
    - The GPIO pin pa5 is configured as a push-pull output to control the LED.
    - The set_high and set_low methods toggle the LED.

RTIC Framework

The Real-Time Interrupt-driven Concurrency (RTIC) framework provides a structured way to write multitasking embedded applications. Below is an example:

```rust
#![no_main]
#![no_std]


use rtic::app;


#[app(device = stm32f4xx_hal::pac)]
mod app {

    #[resources]

    struct Resources {

        // Shared resources

    }


    #[init]

    fn init(_: init::Context) {

        // Initialization code

    }


    #[idle]
```

```
fn idle(_: idle::Context) -> ! {

    loop {

        // Idle loop

    }

}

}
```

Simulating Embedded Systems

Rust provides tools like QEMU for simulating embedded systems on your PC. This is useful for testing code before deploying it to hardware.

Conclusion

Rust's capabilities extend seamlessly into game development and embedded systems, two fields that demand high performance and reliability. With libraries like Bevy and frameworks like RTIC, developers can build robust, scalable applications tailored to their needs. As Rust's ecosystem continues to grow, its influence in these domains is set to expand, providing modern tools and techniques to solve complex challenges.

Chapter 9: Optimizing Rust Programs

Performance Tuning and Profiling

Performance optimization in Rust involves understanding your program's behavior, identifying bottlenecks, and applying targeted improvements. Rust provides a rich set of tools and techniques for analyzing performance and fine-tuning applications to achieve maximum efficiency.

Understanding Performance Bottlenecks

Before diving into optimization, it's essential to identify the areas in your code that consume the most resources. Common bottlenecks include:

- **Hot Loops**: Loops that perform significant computation or operate on large datasets repeatedly.
- **Memory Allocation**: Excessive or inefficient memory usage can slow down your program.
- **Synchronization Overhead**: When using multithreading, locks and other synchronization primitives can introduce delays.

Profiling tools help pinpoint these bottlenecks, making optimization more targeted and efficient.

Profiling Tools in Rust

Rust integrates well with a variety of profiling tools. Some of the most commonly used are:

1. `perf` **(Linux)**: A powerful command-line tool for performance analysis.
2. `cargo-flamegraph`: Generates a visual representation of where your program spends most of its time.
3. `valgrind`: Useful for detecting memory leaks and profiling memory usage.
4. `heaptrack`: Specialized in analyzing heap allocations.

Example: Using `cargo-flamegraph`

To install and use `cargo-flamegraph`, follow these steps:

Install   the   tool:
bash

```
cargo install flamegraph
```

   1.

Run your program with `cargo flamegraph`:
bash

```
cargo flamegraph
```

2.
3. Analyze the generated SVG file to identify hotspots.

Optimizing Hot Loops

Once you've identified a hot loop, consider the following strategies for optimization:

1. **Minimize Work Per Iteration**: Move calculations outside the loop whenever possible.
2. **Use Iterators**: Rust's iterators are often more efficient than manual looping.
3. **Parallelize Where Appropriate**: Leverage crates like `rayon` to parallelize computationally intensive loops.

Example: Optimizing a Hot Loop

```rust
fn sum_squares(nums: &[i32]) -> i32 {

    nums.iter().map(|&x| x * x).sum()

}
```

```rust
// Optimized with Rayon for parallelism

use rayon::prelude::*;


fn sum_squares_parallel(nums: &[i32]) -> i32 {

    nums.par_iter().map(|&x| x * x).sum()

}
```

In this example, the `rayon` crate transforms a sequential operation into a parallel one, which can significantly reduce runtime on multi-core processors.

Managing Memory Efficiently

Memory management is a critical factor in performance. Rust's ownership model helps prevent many common memory issues, but there are still best practices to follow:

1. **Use Stack Allocation When Possible**: The stack is faster than the heap for allocation and deallocation.
2. **Avoid Unnecessary Cloning**: Cloning can be expensive, so consider borrowing (&) or moving (Box, Rc, Arc) data instead.
3. **Profile Allocations**: Tools like heaptrack can show where your program allocates memory.

Example: Avoiding Unnecessary Clones

```
// Inefficient

let v = vec![1, 2, 3];

let v_clone = v.clone();

println!("{:?}", v_clone);
```

```
// Efficient

let v = vec![1, 2, 3];

println!("{:?}", &v);
```

Leveraging Compiler Optimizations

The Rust compiler (rustc) performs various optimizations by default, but you can tweak the build settings for better performance.

Build Profiles

Rust has two primary build profiles:

- **Debug**: Optimized for fast compilation and debuggability.
- **Release**: Optimized for performance.

Always build with the --release flag for production:

```
cargo build --release
```

Inline Functions

Small, frequently called functions can benefit from inlining:

```rust
#[inline]
fn add(a: i32, b: i32) -> i32 {
    a + b
}
```

Writing Idiomatic Rust Code

Writing idiomatic Rust often leads to better performance due to its close alignment with the language's underlying principles.

1. **Use Slices and References**: Prefer slices (`&[T]`) over owned collections (`Vec<T>`) when possible.
2. **Choose the Right Data Structures**: Use hash maps, B-trees, or linked lists based on the workload's requirements.
3. **Avoid Unnecessary Abstractions**: Overuse of traits or dynamic dispatch can introduce performance overhead.

Example: Using Slices

```rust
fn process_data(data: &[i32]) {
    for num in data {
        println!("{}", num);
    }
}
```

Conclusion

Performance tuning in Rust is a systematic process that begins with profiling to identify bottlenecks, followed by targeted optimization. By leveraging Rust's ecosystem of tools and adhering to best practices, you can build applications that are both efficient and maintainable. Remember, the goal is not premature optimization but achieving a balance between performance, readability, and maintainability.

Memory Management Best Practices

Effective memory management is a cornerstone of building performant and robust applications in Rust. Rust's ownership system provides guarantees of safety, but achieving optimal performance often requires understanding how memory is allocated, used, and freed. This section explores best practices and techniques to manage memory efficiently in Rust, focusing on stack and heap usage, avoiding common pitfalls, and leveraging Rust's features to minimize overhead.

Stack vs. Heap Allocation

Rust distinguishes between stack and heap memory, each serving specific purposes:

1. **Stack**:
   - Fast allocation and deallocation.
   - Suitable for fixed-size data and small allocations.
   - Automatically cleaned up when the scope ends.
2. **Heap**:
   - Allows dynamic memory allocation.
   - Suitable for large or variable-size data.
   - Requires explicit management (handled by Rust's ownership and borrowing system).

Example: Stack Allocation

```
fn calculate_sum(a: i32, b: i32) -> i32 {

    a + b // Both `a` and `b` are stored on the stack.

}
```

Example: Heap Allocation

```
fn create_vector() -> Vec<i32> {

    let v = vec![1, 2, 3]; // Allocated on the heap.
```

```
                v

}
```

Avoiding Excessive Cloning

Cloning is a common source of inefficiency in Rust programs. While cloning is sometimes necessary, excessive use can lead to performance degradation due to unnecessary heap allocations.

Strategies to Avoid Cloning

1. Use **references** (&T) instead of owned types.
2. Use **shared ownership** (Rc<T> or Arc<T>) when multiple entities need access to the same data.
3. Opt for **borrowed slices** (&[T]) or strings (&str) over owned collections (Vec<T> or String).

Example: Avoiding Cloning

```rust
// Inefficient: Cloning the vector

fn process_data_cloned(data: Vec<i32>) {

    let cloned_data = data.clone();

    println!("{:?}", cloned_data);

}


// Efficient: Using a reference

fn process_data_ref(data: &[i32]) {

    println!("{:?}", data);

}
```

Efficient Data Structures

Choosing the right data structure can significantly impact memory usage and performance. Rust offers a wide range of standard and third-party data structures tailored to different workloads.

Common Data Structures

1. **Vectors (Vec<T>)**: Dynamic arrays for contiguous memory storage.
2. **Hash Maps (HashMap<K, V>)**: Key-value storage optimized for fast lookups.
3. **B-Trees (BTreeMap<K, V>)**: Ordered key-value storage with efficient range queries.
4. **Strings (String, &str)**: Managed and borrowed string types.

Example: Using HashMap vs. BTreeMap

```rust
use std::collections::{HashMap, BTreeMap};


fn compare_maps() {

    let mut hash_map = HashMap::new();

    let mut btree_map = BTreeMap::new();


    hash_map.insert("key1", 10);

    btree_map.insert("key1", 10);


    println!("HashMap: {:?}", hash_map);

    println!("BTreeMap: {:?}", btree_map);

}
```

Memory Reuse with Pools

For workloads involving frequent allocation and deallocation of objects, memory pooling can reduce overhead and fragmentation. A memory pool allows reusing allocated memory instead of creating new allocations every time.

Example: Using typed_arena Crate

```
# Add to Cargo.toml

[dependencies]

typed-arena = "2.0"
```

```
use typed_arena::Arena;


fn main() {

    let arena = Arena::new();

    let value = arena.alloc(42); // Memory is allocated from the pool.

    println!("Value: {}", value);

}
```

Avoiding Dangling References

Rust's ownership and borrowing rules prevent most dangling reference issues. However, improper use of unsafe code or external libraries can lead to undefined behavior.

Safe Example

```
fn safe_reference() {

    let s = String::from("hello");

    let r = &s; // Borrowing is safe and managed.

    println!("{}", r);

}
```

Unsafe Example (Avoid This)

```
fn dangling_pointer() {

    let r;

    {

        let s = String::from("hello");

        r = &s; // `s` goes out of scope here.

    }

    // println!("{}", r); // This would cause a compile-time error.

}
```

Memory Leaks and Their Avoidance

While Rust ensures that memory is freed when it goes out of scope, memory leaks can occur when reference cycles are created using Rc or Arc.

Avoiding Reference Cycles

Use Weak references to break cycles:

```
use std::rc::{Rc, Weak};


struct Node {

    value: i32,

    next: Option<Rc<Node>>,

    prev: Option<Weak<Node>>,

}
```

```rust
fn main() {
    let node1 = Rc::new(Node {
        value: 1,
        next: None,
        prev: None,
    });

    let node2 = Rc::new(Node {
        value: 2,
        next: Some(node1.clone()),
        prev: Some(Rc::downgrade(&node1)),
    });

    // No memory leaks despite circular references.
}
```

Leveraging Box for Heap Allocation

When stack memory is insufficient, use Box<T> to allocate objects on the heap. This is particularly useful for recursive data structures.

Example: Recursive Data Structure

```rust
enum List {
    Node(i32, Box<List>),
    Nil,
}
```

```
fn main() {

    let     list    =     List::Node(1,     Box::new(List::Node(2,
Box::new(List::Nil))));

}
```

Conclusion

Memory management in Rust is both a science and an art. By understanding stack and heap allocation, minimizing unnecessary cloning, choosing efficient data structures, and leveraging tools like memory pools, you can build programs that are both performant and safe. Rust's ownership model provides a strong foundation, but applying these best practices ensures you make the most of what the language has to offer.

Writing Idiomatic Rust Code

Writing idiomatic Rust code is about embracing the language's unique features and paradigms to create clean, efficient, and maintainable software. Idiomatic code not only aligns with the community's best practices but also leverages Rust's design principles to maximize performance and safety. This section explores key guidelines and patterns to help you write idiomatic Rust code.

Ownership and Borrowing

Rust's ownership model is central to its safety guarantees. Writing idiomatic code means understanding and effectively using ownership, borrowing, and lifetimes.

Prefer Borrowing Over Cloning

Instead of duplicating data unnecessarily, borrow references whenever possible. This reduces memory usage and avoids additional heap allocations.

```
fn print_vector(data: &[i32]) {

    for item in data {

        println!("{}", item);

    }

}
```

```rust
fn main() {

    let numbers = vec![1, 2, 3, 4];

    print_vector(&numbers); // Borrow instead of cloning the vector

}
```

Use Lifetimes to Manage References

Lifetimes explicitly define how long references are valid, preventing dangling references and ensuring memory safety.

```rust
fn longest<'a>(x: &'a str, y: &'a str) -> &'a str {

    if x.len() > y.len() {

        x

    } else {

        y

    }

}


fn main() {

    let s1 = String::from("hello");

    let s2 = String::from("world!");

    println!("The longest string is {}", longest(&s1, &s2));

}
```

Error Handling

Rust encourages robust error handling using the `Result` and `Option` enums, rather than relying on exceptions.

Avoid Panic in Idiomatic Code

Idiomatic Rust reserves `panic!` for unrecoverable errors. Use `Result` for recoverable errors and propagate them using the `?` operator.

```rust
fn read_file(filename: &str) -> std::io::Result<String> {

    std::fs::read_to_string(filename)

}
```

```rust
fn main() -> std::io::Result<()> {

    let content = read_file("example.txt")?;

    println!("{}", content);

    Ok(())

}
```

Use `match` for Comprehensive Handling

Use `match` statements to handle all possible outcomes explicitly, making your code safer and more predictable.

```rust
fn divide(a: i32, b: i32) -> Option<i32> {

    if b == 0 {

        None

    } else {

        Some(a / b)

    }
```

```
}

fn main() {

    match divide(10, 2) {

        Some(result) => println!("Result: {}", result),

        None => println!("Cannot divide by zero"),

    }

}
```

Structuring Code with Modules and Crates

Organizing code into modules and crates makes it more maintainable and reusable.

Define Modules for Logical Grouping

Use modules to group related functionality and expose only necessary components.

```
mod math {

    pub fn add(a: i32, b: i32) -> i32 {

        a + b

    }


    fn subtract(a: i32, b: i32) -> i32 {

        a - b

    }

}


fn main() {
```

```
    println!("Sum: {}", math::add(5, 3));

}
```

Use Crates for Dependency Management

The Rust ecosystem relies heavily on crates. Use `Cargo.toml` to manage dependencies and avoid reinventing the wheel.

```
[dependencies]

rand = "0.8"
```

```
use rand::Rng;

fn main() {

    let mut rng = rand::thread_rng();

    let random_number: i32 = rng.gen_range(1..101);

    println!("Random number: {}", random_number);

}
```

Traits and Generics

Traits and generics allow for flexible and reusable code by abstracting over shared behavior.

Implement Traits for Shared Behavior

Traits define a contract for types, ensuring they implement specific methods.

```
trait Greet {
```

```rust
    fn greet(&self);

}


struct Person {

    name: String,

}


impl Greet for Person {

    fn greet(&self) {

        println!("Hello, my name is {}", self.name);

    }

}


fn main() {

    let person = Person { name: String::from("Alice") };

    person.greet();

}
```

Use Generics for Type Flexibility

Generics allow functions and structs to operate on multiple data types without sacrificing type safety.

```rust
fn largest<T: PartialOrd>(list: &[T]) -> &T {

    let mut largest = &list[0];

    for item in list.iter() {
```

```rust
        if item > largest {

            largest = item;

        }

    }

    largest

}


fn main() {

    let numbers = vec![3, 5, 2, 8];

    println!("The largest number is {}", largest(&numbers));

}
```

Functional Programming Idioms

Rust embraces functional programming features, such as closures, iterators, and pattern matching.

Use Closures for Inline Behavior

Closures are anonymous functions that capture variables from their environment.

```rust
fn apply<F>(f: F)

where

    F: Fn(i32) -> i32,

{

    let result = f(10);

    println!("Result: {}", result);

}
```

```rust
fn main() {
    let square = |x: i32| x * x;

    apply(square);
}
```

Chain Iterators for Declarative Code

Iterators provide a concise and expressive way to manipulate collections.

```rust
fn main() {
    let numbers = vec![1, 2, 3, 4, 5];

    let squares: Vec<_> = numbers.iter().map(|x| x * x).collect();

    println!("{:?}", squares);
}
```

Leveraging Community Best Practices

Idiomatic Rust is not just about language syntax but also about aligning with the broader Rust community's conventions.

Follow Rustfmt for Consistent Formatting

Use rustfmt to automatically format your code according to the community's style guidelines.

```
cargo fmt
```

Clippy for Linting

Use clippy to catch common mistakes and improve code quality.

```
cargo clippy
```

Conclusion

Writing idiomatic Rust code involves understanding and leveraging the language's unique features, including ownership, traits, and functional programming paradigms. By following these best practices, you can create code that is not only efficient and safe but also clean and maintainable, aligning with the broader Rust community standards. Idiomatic Rust encourages clarity, safety, and performance, making it a pleasure to write and maintain over time.

Chapter 10: Rust and Beyond

Interfacing with Other Languages

Rust's powerful combination of safety, performance, and expressiveness makes it an excellent choice for integrating with other programming languages. Whether you are adding Rust to an existing codebase or building a new project that needs interoperability with C, Python, JavaScript, or other languages, Rust provides robust tools and patterns for seamless integration.

Understanding Foreign Function Interface (FFI)

The Foreign Function Interface (FFI) is a critical component in enabling Rust to interact with code written in other languages. Rust's unsafe keyword allows the use of FFI for low-level interoperation, while ensuring you explicitly acknowledge the potential risks.

Key Rust tools for FFI include:

- `extern` **blocks**: Define external functions in Rust that are implemented in another language.
- `#[no_mangle]` **attribute**: Ensures the Rust compiler does not alter the function name during compilation, maintaining compatibility.
- `libc` **crate**: Provides definitions for common C libraries and system calls.

Example: Calling a C Function from Rust

```rust
#[link(name = "mylib")]

extern "C" {

    fn c_function(arg: i32) -> i32;

}


fn main() {

    unsafe {

        let result = c_function(42);

        println!("Result from C: {}", result);
```

```
    }

}
```

In this example, the Rust program links to a C library named `mylib` and invokes a function `c_function` declared in that library.

Rust and C Interoperability

C is one of the most common languages Rust interacts with due to its widespread use in systems programming. Rust can seamlessly call C functions and be called from C code, making it an ideal candidate for incrementally replacing legacy C components in large systems.

Creating a C-compatible Rust Library

To create a Rust library that can be called from C:

1. Use the `#[no_mangle]` attribute on functions.
2. Ensure function signatures use `extern "C"` to match C's ABI.
3. Export symbols in the Cargo build process.

Example: Exposing Rust Functions to C

```rust
#[no_mangle]

pub extern "C" fn add(a: i32, b: i32) -> i32 {

    a + b

}
```

Compile this code into a shared library (e.g., `.so` or `.dll`), which can then be linked from C code.

Safety Considerations

When working with FFI:

- **Memory Ownership**: Clearly define which language owns allocated memory.
- **Data Types**: Ensure data structures are compatible between Rust and the foreign language.
- **Error Handling**: Translate errors across language boundaries.

Interfacing with Python

Python, being an interpreted and dynamically-typed language, complements Rust's performance and type safety. Rust can serve as a backend for performance-critical Python applications.

Using the pyo3 Crate

The pyo3 crate simplifies Python-Rust integration. It allows you to write Python extensions in Rust and call Rust code from Python.

Example: Creating a Python Module in Rust

Add pyo3 to your Cargo.toml:

```toml
[dependencies]
pyo3 = { version = "0.18", features = ["extension-module"] }
```

Write the Rust code:

```rust
use pyo3::prelude::*;


#[pyfunction]

fn sum_numbers(a: i32, b: i32) -> i32 {

    a + b

}


#[pymodule]

fn my_rust_module(py: Python, m: &PyModule) -> PyResult<()> {

    m.add_function(wrap_pyfunction!(sum_numbers, m)?)?;

    Ok(())
```

```
}
```

Compile the module as a Python-compatible shared library. You can then use it in Python:

```python
import my_rust_module


result = my_rust_module.sum_numbers(10, 20)
print("Sum:", result)
```

Rust and JavaScript (Wasm)

Rust's WebAssembly (Wasm) capabilities make it a popular choice for enhancing JavaScript applications. Rust can compile to Wasm, allowing you to run Rust code in web browsers.

Using the `wasm-bindgen` Crate

The `wasm-bindgen` crate bridges Rust and JavaScript, enabling bi-directional communication.

Example: Rust Function in JavaScript

Add `wasm-bindgen` to your `Cargo.toml`:

```toml
[dependencies]
wasm-bindgen = "0.2"
```

Write the Rust code:

```rust
use wasm_bindgen::prelude::*;


#[wasm_bindgen]
```

```rust
pub fn greet(name: &str) -> String {

    format!("Hello, {}!", name)

}
```

Compile the Rust code to Wasm using `wasm-pack`, and then use it in JavaScript:

```javascript
import { greet } from './pkg';


console.log(greet('World'));
```

Bridging Rust with Other Languages

Rust's interoperability extends to many other languages, including:

- **Java**: Using JNI (Java Native Interface).
- **C#**: Through P/Invoke or FFI libraries.
- **Go**: Via C bindings or plugins.

Conclusion

Interfacing Rust with other languages opens new horizons for performance optimization, system integration, and extending existing projects. Rust's FFI capabilities and ecosystem tools make it easier to adopt Rust incrementally, enabling developers to combine Rust's strengths with the unique features of other languages. By leveraging Rust in a multi-language environment, you can create robust, high-performance, and maintainable software.

Future Trends and Innovations in Rust

Rust has firmly established itself as a leading language in systems programming, but its potential extends far beyond its current applications. As technology evolves, Rust is poised to play a critical role in shaping future innovations across various domains. This section explores emerging trends and future directions in the Rust ecosystem, focusing on its growth in safety-critical systems, artificial intelligence, cloud computing, and beyond.

Rust in Safety-Critical Systems

Safety-critical systems, such as those used in aerospace, automotive, and healthcare industries, require the utmost reliability and performance. Rust's unique combination of memory safety and concurrency guarantees makes it an excellent candidate for these environments.

Adoption in Embedded Systems

Embedded systems often face stringent resource constraints and require precise control over hardware. Rust's low-level capabilities and abstractions provide an ideal balance between performance and developer productivity. The `embedded-hal` and `no_std` ecosystems in Rust support the development of embedded applications without requiring the full standard library.

Example: Basic Embedded Application

```rust
#![no_std]
#![no_main]


use cortex_m_rt::entry;


#[entry]
fn main() -> ! {
    loop {
        // Toggle an LED or interact with hardware
    }
}
```

Certification for Critical Use Cases

Efforts are underway to make Rust compliant with standards like ISO 26262 for automotive safety and DO-178C for aerospace. These certifications will open new avenues for Rust in regulated industries.

The Role of Rust in Artificial Intelligence

While Python dominates the AI landscape, Rust offers unique advantages for performance-critical AI applications. Its ability to manage memory safely and efficiently positions it as a promising choice for AI and machine learning (ML) frameworks.

Accelerating AI Workflows

Rust-based AI libraries, such as `tch-rs` (bindings for PyTorch) and `ndarray`, allow developers to write high-performance ML models. Moreover, Rust can complement Python by serving as a backend for computationally intensive tasks.

Example: Using Rust for AI Computations

```rust
use ndarray::Array;


fn main() {

    let a = Array::from_vec(vec![1.0, 2.0, 3.0]);

    let b = Array::from_vec(vec![4.0, 5.0, 6.0]);


    let dot_product = a.dot(&b);

    println!("Dot Product: {}", dot_product);

}
```

Emerging Rust ML Frameworks

Projects like `huggingface/tokenizers` and `rust-bert` showcase Rust's growing influence in AI. These frameworks aim to provide fast, reliable alternatives to existing Python tools.

Rust in Cloud Computing and Web Assembly

The rise of serverless architectures and edge computing has created demand for efficient, lightweight, and secure programming models. Rust's ability to compile to WebAssembly (Wasm) and its thriving ecosystem for cloud-native tools make it an excellent choice for modern cloud computing needs.

WebAssembly: Rust at the Edge

Rust is one of the leading languages for compiling to WebAssembly, enabling high-performance applications to run in browsers, on the server, or at the edge.

Example: Basic Wasm Cloud Function

```rust
use wasm_bindgen::prelude::*;


#[wasm_bindgen]

pub fn process_data(input: &str) -> String {

    format!("Processed: {}", input)

}
```

Deploying Wasm modules in serverless platforms like Cloudflare Workers or Fastly is becoming increasingly common, leveraging Rust's speed and security.

Cloud-Native Tools in Rust

Rust-based tools like `tokio` (asynchronous programming) and `actix-web` (web framework) have gained traction in cloud-native application development. These libraries enable the creation of robust and scalable systems with minimal resource overhead.

Innovations in Programming Paradigms

Rust's community continues to explore and implement innovative paradigms, pushing the boundaries of what the language can achieve.

Zero-Cost Abstractions and Async Evolution

Rust's zero-cost abstractions ensure that high-level constructs do not incur runtime overhead. The evolution of the `async` ecosystem, including the stabilization of features like `async fn in traits`, will further enhance Rust's ability to handle complex asynchronous workflows.

Example: Async Trait in Rust

```rust
use async_trait::async_trait;
```

```
#[async_trait]

trait DataFetcher {

    async fn fetch(&self) -> String;

}


struct WebFetcher;


#[async_trait]

impl DataFetcher for WebFetcher {

    async fn fetch(&self) -> String {

        "Data from the web".to_string()

    }

}
```

Functional Programming in Rust

Rust's type system supports functional programming patterns, such as immutability and higher-order functions. Libraries like `fp-core` are bringing advanced functional programming concepts to the language.

Community Growth and Open Source Contributions

The Rust community has been a driving force behind its rapid growth. Collaborative efforts across industries, academia, and open source projects continue to fuel innovation.

Key Community Trends

- **Diversity and Inclusion**: Initiatives to broaden the Rust community's demographic reach.
- **Education and Training**: Comprehensive resources, such as `rustlings` and the Rust Book, ensure accessibility for new developers.
- **Corporate Adoption**: Companies like Microsoft, Amazon, and Google are actively contributing to Rust development.

Rust and Quantum Computing

Rust's strong type system and compile-time guarantees make it a potential candidate for quantum computing libraries. While still in its infancy, research into Rust-based quantum programming is gaining momentum.

Example: Quantum Simulation

Though highly experimental, libraries like `qrusty` explore quantum computing paradigms using Rust.

The Future of Rust Tooling

Improved tooling, such as Rust Analyzer, will continue to enhance developer productivity. Features like error diagnostics, automatic code fixes, and performance analysis are set to evolve further.

Conclusion

Rust's future is bright, with innovations spanning across domains such as safety-critical systems, AI, cloud computing, and more. Its robust ecosystem, coupled with a vibrant and inclusive community, ensures that Rust will remain a key player in shaping the next generation of software development. By staying ahead of technological trends, Rust promises to unlock new possibilities for developers worldwide.

Community Contributions and Open Source Projects

The Rust programming language owes much of its success to its vibrant and engaged community. Through open source projects, collaborative development, and a shared commitment to innovation, the Rust ecosystem continues to grow and thrive. This section explores the role of the Rust community, highlights notable open source projects, and provides guidance on how to contribute to Rust's ecosystem effectively.

The Rust Community: A Collaborative Ecosystem

One of Rust's defining features is its welcoming and inclusive community. From the earliest days of the language's development, fostering a collaborative environment has been a core priority. The Rust community comprises developers, maintainers, educators, and advocates who contribute in various ways to the language's evolution.

The Rust Governance Model

The Rust project employs a unique governance model based on working groups and teams. Key teams include:

- **Core Team**: Oversees the direction of the Rust language and its ecosystem.
- **Compiler Team**: Focuses on improving the Rust compiler (`rustc`).
- **Library Team**: Manages the Rust standard library.

- **Community Team**: Promotes outreach, events, and education.
- **Docs Team**: Maintains the Rust documentation and ensures it is accessible to users of all levels.

This decentralized model allows for community-driven decision-making while maintaining a cohesive vision for Rust.

Notable Open Source Projects in the Rust Ecosystem

The Rust ecosystem is home to a diverse array of open source projects, ranging from foundational tools to innovative applications. These projects demonstrate Rust's versatility and its ability to address real-world challenges.

Servo: A High-Performance Browser Engine

Servo is an experimental browser engine developed by Mozilla to demonstrate how Rust's safety and concurrency features can revolutionize web technology. Written entirely in Rust, Servo aims to be secure, fast, and modular.

Key Features:

- Parallel layout and rendering.
- Memory safety to prevent common vulnerabilities like use-after-free errors.
- Modular architecture for extensibility.

Developers can explore Servo as an example of how Rust can be applied to large-scale, complex systems.

ripgrep: A Fast Search Tool

ripgrep is a command-line utility for searching files that combines the functionality of tools like grep and ag. Built for speed and accuracy, it leverages Rust's performance and safe concurrency.

Usage Example:

```
rg "search_term" path/to/directory
```

The tool is widely adopted in the developer community and showcases how Rust can produce efficient, user-friendly command-line applications.

tokio: Asynchronous Runtime for Rust

Tokio is a high-performance asynchronous runtime designed to build fast and reliable network applications. It serves as the foundation for numerous web servers, microservices, and networked applications in the Rust ecosystem.

Example: Simple TCP Server Using Tokio

```rust
use tokio::net::TcpListener;

use tokio::io::{AsyncReadExt, AsyncWriteExt};


#[tokio::main]

async fn main() -> Result<(), Box<dyn std::error::Error>> {

    let listener = TcpListener::bind("127.0.0.1:8080").await?;


    loop {

        let (mut socket, _) = listener.accept().await?;

        tokio::spawn(async move {

            let mut buf = [0; 1024];

            if let Ok(n) = socket.read(&mut buf).await {

                socket.write_all(&buf[0..n]).await.unwrap();

            }

        });

    }

}
```

This snippet demonstrates how developers can build scalable network services using Tokio's primitives.

Bevy: A Rust Game Engine

Bevy is an open source game engine built in Rust that emphasizes simplicity and productivity. Its modular architecture and support for modern game development workflows make it an excellent choice for creating 2D and 3D games.

Features:

- Entity-component-system (ECS) architecture.
- Hot reloading for assets.
- Cross-platform support.

Developers can contribute to Bevy or use it as a foundation for their game development projects.

Getting Involved in the Rust Ecosystem

Contributing to Rust and its ecosystem provides an opportunity to learn, grow, and make a meaningful impact on the programming world.

How to Contribute

1. **Choose an Area of Interest**: Decide whether you want to work on the compiler, standard library, documentation, or an external library.
2. **Find Open Issues**: Use platforms like GitHub to discover issues tagged with `good first issue` or `help wanted`.
3. **Engage with the Community**: Join forums, Discord channels, and Rust conferences to connect with other contributors.
4. **Submit Pull Requests**: Start small by fixing bugs or adding documentation before moving on to larger contributions.

Tools and Resources for Contributors

- **Rust Playground**: Experiment with Rust code directly in your browser.
- **Rustup**: Manage Rust versions and toolchains.
- **Clippy**: A linting tool to enforce Rust best practices.
- **cargo-expand**: Visualize expanded macros for better debugging.

Supporting the Rust Community

Beyond code contributions, there are many ways to support the Rust community:

- **Write Tutorials and Blog Posts**: Share your knowledge and experiences with Rust.
- **Organize Meetups and Workshops**: Build local communities and promote Rust adoption.
- **Sponsor Development**: Financially support Rust projects through platforms like Open Collective or GitHub Sponsors.

The Future of Open Source in Rust

Rust's open source nature ensures its long-term sustainability and adaptability. As the community grows, we can expect:

- Increased adoption in new industries.
- More diverse contributors bringing fresh perspectives.

- Continued innovation driven by collaboration.

Conclusion

Community contributions and open source projects are the lifeblood of Rust. They drive innovation, foster learning, and ensure the language remains accessible and relevant. By participating in the Rust ecosystem, developers can not only enhance their skills but also shape the future of software development. Whether you're a seasoned expert or a newcomer, there is a place for you in the Rust community.

Chapter 11: Conclusion

Reflecting on Rust's Strengths

Rust has become a prominent language in the world of programming, gaining widespread recognition for its unique approach to solving long-standing challenges in software development. Its design choices, though at times demanding, have enabled developers to write highly efficient, safe, and concurrent code. This section reflects on the strengths of Rust that make it a standout choice for modern software engineering.

Safety Without Sacrificing Performance

At the heart of Rust's philosophy is its focus on safety. Unlike traditional systems programming languages such as C or C++, Rust provides compile-time guarantees that prevent common pitfalls like null pointer dereferences, use-after-free errors, and data races. This is achieved through features like ownership, borrowing, and the strict enforcement of lifetimes. These concepts are not merely academic—they empower developers to build reliable systems without relying on a garbage collector or runtime checks.

For example, consider a scenario where you manage a shared resource across multiple threads. In Rust, the borrow checker ensures that only one thread can modify the resource at a time while others may read it. This eliminates the need for manual lock management and prevents subtle bugs:

```rust
use std::sync::{Arc, Mutex};
use std::thread;


fn main() {
    let data = Arc::new(Mutex::new(0));


    let mut handles = vec![];


    for _ in 0..10 {
        let data_clone = Arc::clone(&data);
        let handle = thread::spawn(move || {
```

```
        let mut num = data_clone.lock().unwrap();

        *num += 1;

    });

    handles.push(handle);

}


for handle in handles {

    handle.join().unwrap();

}


println!("Final count: {}", *data.lock().unwrap());

}
```

In this example, the `Mutex` ensures safe concurrent access, while the `Arc` type provides shared ownership. Such patterns are straightforward in Rust, and the compiler enforces their correct usage, removing ambiguity and reducing debugging overhead.

Expressive Type System

Rust's type system is another cornerstone of its strength. With features like generics, traits, and enums, the language allows developers to express complex ideas succinctly while maintaining clarity. This expressiveness is particularly valuable in scenarios where domain-specific constraints need to be modeled directly in the type system.

For instance, enums in Rust go beyond simple variants—they can encapsulate data, making them ideal for representing state transitions or polymorphic behavior:

```
enum PaymentStatus {

    Pending,

    Completed { amount: f64 },
```

```rust
        Failed(String),

}


fn process_payment(status: PaymentStatus) {

    match status {

        PaymentStatus::Pending    =>    println!("Payment    is    still
pending."),

        PaymentStatus::Completed { amount } => println!("Payment of
${} completed.", amount),

        PaymentStatus::Failed(reason) => println!("Payment failed due
to: {}", reason),

    }

}


fn main() {

    let status = PaymentStatus::Completed { amount: 150.0 };

    process_payment(status);

}
```

This example demonstrates how Rust enables developers to model real-world scenarios intuitively. The strong typing ensures that edge cases, such as unhandled states, are caught during compilation rather than at runtime.

Concurrency Without Fear

Concurrency is one of the most challenging aspects of modern programming. Rust's ownership system extends to its concurrency model, providing a solid foundation for writing parallel and concurrent applications without fear of data races.

Rust's Send and Sync traits play a critical role here. They ensure that data can be safely shared or transferred across threads, and the compiler enforces these guarantees at compile time. This eliminates runtime surprises and fosters confidence in multi-threaded code.

Here's an example of parallel computation using Rust's `std::thread` module:

```rust
use std::thread;

fn main() {
    let data = vec![1, 2, 3, 4, 5];

    let handles: Vec<_> = data.into_iter().map(|x| {
        thread::spawn(move || x * 2)
    }).collect();

    for handle in handles {
        let result = handle.join().unwrap();
        println!("Result: {}", result);
    }
}
```

In this case, each thread processes a portion of the data independently. The ownership system ensures that each thread has its own copy of the data, avoiding conflicts or unexpected behavior.

Ecosystem and Tooling

Rust's ecosystem is another aspect worth highlighting. The `Cargo` package manager and build system make dependency management and project setup seamless. With a single command, developers can create a new project, add dependencies, and build or test their code.

Additionally, Rust's community has contributed a wealth of high-quality libraries, often referred to as "crates." These libraries cover a wide range of domains, from web development and data processing to game development and embedded systems. The vibrant ecosystem fosters innovation and collaboration, enabling developers to focus on solving problems rather than reinventing the wheel.

Developer Experience

While Rust's learning curve can be steep, the language's focus on developer experience is evident. The compiler provides detailed error messages, often including suggestions for fixing issues. This feedback loop helps developers understand and adopt Rust's principles more effectively.

For instance, encountering an error like this:

```
error[E0382]: borrow of moved value: `x`
  --> main.rs:10:15
   |
8  |      let x = vec![1, 2, 3];
   |          - move occurs because `x` has type `Vec<i32>`, which does
not implement the `Copy` trait
9  |      let y = x;
10 |      println!("{:?}", x);
   |                       ^ value borrowed here after move
```

Guides developers to understand ownership and borrowing mechanics. The compiler acts as an educator, reinforcing best practices and preventing potential bugs.

Conclusion

Rust's strengths lie in its ability to tackle modern software development challenges with innovative solutions. By prioritizing safety, performance, and expressiveness, Rust has redefined what's possible in systems programming. Its ecosystem, tooling, and community support ensure that developers have the resources they need to succeed.

As we reflect on these strengths, it's clear that Rust is more than just a programming language—it's a paradigm shift that empowers developers to write code that is not only correct and efficient but also maintainable and future-proof.

Continuing Your Rust Journey

Learning Rust is not just about mastering its syntax and semantics; it's a gateway to developing a deeper understanding of programming principles. This section focuses on practical steps, best practices, and resources to help you grow as a Rust developer and make the most out of the language.

Build Real-World Projects

The best way to solidify your knowledge of Rust is by building projects that solve real problems. Start with simple applications and gradually work your way up to more complex systems. Here are a few project ideas to get started:

- **CLI Tools**: Create command-line tools using the `clap` or `structopt` crate for argument parsing.
- **Web Applications**: Build a small REST API using frameworks like Actix or Rocket.
- **Game Development**: Experiment with 2D or 3D game engines like `ggez` or `bevy`.
- **Embedded Systems**: Use Rust for programming microcontrollers or low-level hardware.

For example, a simple CLI tool to manage tasks might look like this:

```rust
use std::collections::HashMap;

use std::env;


fn main() {

    let mut tasks = HashMap::new();

    tasks.insert(1, "Learn Rust".to_string());

    tasks.insert(2, "Write a blog post".to_string());


    let args: Vec<String> = env::args().collect();

    if args.len() < 2 {

        println!("Usage: task_manager <list|add|remove>");

        return;

    }
```

```rust
match args[1].as_str() {
    "list" => {
        for (id, task) in &tasks {
            println!("{}: {}", id, task);
        }
    }
    "add" => {
        if args.len() < 3 {
            println!("Usage: task_manager add <task>");
            return;
        }
        let task_id = tasks.len() + 1;
        tasks.insert(task_id, args[2].clone());
        println!("Added task: {}", args[2]);
    }
    "remove" => {
        if args.len() < 3 {
            println!("Usage: task_manager remove <task_id>");
            return;
        }
        let task_id: usize = args[2].parse().unwrap();
        if tasks.remove(&task_id).is_some() {
            println!("Removed task {}", task_id);
```

```
            } else {

                println!("Task ID not found.");

            }

        }

        _ => println!("Unknown command."),

    }

}
```

This simple application demonstrates Rust's type safety and the power of its standard library. Expanding this project with persistent storage, error handling, or a GUI can serve as an excellent learning exercise.

Engage with the Rust Community

Rust has one of the most welcoming and active programming communities. Engaging with the community can accelerate your learning and connect you with like-minded developers. Here are a few ways to get involved:

- **Forums**: Join the Rust Users Forum to ask questions and share your experiences.
- **Discord**: Participate in discussions on the Rust Programming Language Discord server.
- **Open Source Contributions**: Contribute to popular Rust projects on GitHub. Start with issues labeled good first issue or help wanted.
- **Meetups and Conferences**: Attend Rust-focused events like RustConf or local meetups to network and learn from experts.

By contributing to open source, you not only improve your skills but also give back to the community. For instance, fixing a bug in a crate you use or writing additional documentation can make a significant impact.

Explore Advanced Concepts

Once you are comfortable with Rust's fundamentals, it's time to delve into advanced topics to unlock the full potential of the language. Some areas to explore include:

- **Asynchronous Programming**: Learn how to write non-blocking applications using async/await and the tokio or async-std libraries.
- **Custom Macros**: Create procedural macros to automate repetitive code patterns.
- **Unsafe Rust**: Understand when and how to use unsafe code responsibly for tasks like interfacing with C libraries.

- **Embedded Development**: Explore the `no_std` environment for low-level programming.

For example, here's a small snippet of asynchronous code using `tokio`:

```
use tokio::time::{sleep, Duration};


#[tokio::main]
async fn main() {
    println!("Starting tasks...");

    let task1 = tokio::spawn(async {
        sleep(Duration::from_secs(2)).await;
        println!("Task 1 completed.");
    });

    let task2 = tokio::spawn(async {
        sleep(Duration::from_secs(1)).await;
        println!("Task 2 completed.");
    });

    task1.await.unwrap();
    task2.await.unwrap();

    println!("All tasks completed.");
}
```

This example highlights the power of asynchronous programming in Rust, enabling efficient resource usage and scalability.

Stay Updated

Rust is a rapidly evolving language, with new features and improvements introduced regularly. Staying updated ensures that you remain competitive and leverage the latest advancements. Here are some ways to stay informed:

- **Rust Release Notes**: Review the release notes for each new stable version.
- **Newsletters**: Subscribe to newsletters like "This Week in Rust" for curated updates.
- **Blogs and Tutorials**: Follow blogs from prominent Rust developers to learn about best practices and emerging trends.

Adopt Best Practices

To write idiomatic and maintainable Rust code, adhere to these best practices:

- **Leverage Crates**: Avoid reinventing the wheel by using community libraries whenever possible.
- **Write Tests**: Use Rust's built-in testing framework to write unit and integration tests.
- **Follow the Rust API Guidelines**: Design your APIs with clarity and consistency in mind.
- **Document Your Code**: Use `///` comments for public APIs and `cargo doc` to generate documentation.

Here's a quick example of a simple test:

```rust
fn add(a: i32, b: i32) -> i32 {

    a + b

}



#[cfg(test)]

mod tests {

    use super::*;


    #[test]
```

```
fn test_add() {

    assert_eq!(add(2, 3), 5);

}

}
```

Conclusion

Continuing your Rust journey requires dedication, practice, and community engagement. By building projects, contributing to open source, exploring advanced topics, and adopting best practices, you'll not only enhance your skills but also contribute to the growing ecosystem of Rust developers. Embrace the challenge, and the rewards of mastering Rust will be immense.

Final Thoughts on Mastering Rust

Mastering Rust is not merely an endpoint—it is an ongoing journey that evolves with the language, the projects you build, and the problems you solve. Rust's design philosophy combines pragmatism with innovation, providing a language that bridges low-level system programming and high-level application development. In this section, we will reflect on the broader aspects of Rust mastery, exploring the philosophical underpinnings, practical implications, and future opportunities for Rust developers.

A Philosophy of Ownership

At its core, Rust is more than just syntax and rules—it is a philosophy centered around ownership, responsibility, and precision. The ownership model in Rust is revolutionary, as it teaches developers to think critically about memory and resource management. This philosophy extends beyond programming, fostering habits of clarity and accountability in system design.

Consider the implications of Rust's ownership system:

- **Resource Efficiency**: By enforcing compile-time checks for resource management, Rust ensures that memory, file handles, and other resources are handled responsibly. This reduces runtime overhead and the risk of resource leaks.
- **Data Integrity**: Rust's borrowing rules enforce data integrity, ensuring that no mutable and immutable references coexist in unsafe ways.
- **System Design**: The concepts of ownership and borrowing encourage modular and well-structured code, promoting long-term maintainability.

A simple example demonstrates the clarity of ownership rules:

```rust
fn main() {

    let s = String::from("Hello, Rust!");

    takes_ownership(s); // Ownership of `s` is transferred to the
function

    // println!("{}", s); // This line would cause a compile-time
error


    let x = 10;

    makes_copy(x); // Copy occurs, so `x` is still valid here

    println!("{}", x); // This works because `i32` implements the Copy
trait

}


fn takes_ownership(some_string: String) {

    println!("{}", some_string);

}


fn makes_copy(some_integer: i32) {

    println!("{}", some_integer);

}
```

This example illustrates how Rust enforces clarity in resource management, preventing accidental usage of invalidated data.

Rust in the Real World

Rust's adoption spans diverse domains, from web development to embedded systems, and its application in real-world projects demonstrates its versatility and robustness. Here are a few examples:

- **Web Development**: Frameworks like Actix and Rocket provide high-performance web solutions, while libraries like serde simplify data serialization.
- **Game Development**: Rust's speed and safety make it ideal for building game engines, such as Bevy, which leverage Rust's concurrency model.
- **Embedded Systems**: Rust's no_std mode allows developers to write firmware for microcontrollers, combining safety with performance.

To appreciate Rust's role in real-world applications, consider a basic web server built using Rocket:

```
#[macro_use]

extern crate rocket;


#[get("/")]

fn index() -> &'static str {

    "Welcome to Rust Web Development!"

}


#[launch]

fn rocket() -> _ {

    rocket::build().mount("/", routes![index])

}
```

This simple example demonstrates how Rust's ecosystem enables rapid development while maintaining safety and performance.

The Art of Writing Idiomatic Rust

Idiomatic Rust is about embracing the language's unique features to write clear, efficient, and maintainable code. This involves not just adhering to syntax rules but also leveraging Rust's strengths effectively. Key practices include:

- **Using Enums for State Management**: Rust's enums are powerful tools for representing states and transitions, enabling concise and expressive code.
- **Leveraging Traits for Polymorphism**: Traits provide a way to define shared behavior across types, promoting code reuse and abstraction.
- **Error Handling with Results**: Rust's `Result` and `Option` types provide a structured approach to error handling, avoiding the pitfalls of exceptions.

An idiomatic implementation of a simple state machine might look like this:

```rust
enum DoorState {

    Open,

    Closed,

    Locked,

}



impl DoorState {

    fn open(&self) -> Result<DoorState, &'static str> {

        match self {

            DoorState::Closed => Ok(DoorState::Open),

            DoorState::Locked => Err("Cannot open a locked door"),

            _ => Err("Door is already open"),

        }

    }


    fn close(&self) -> Result<DoorState, &'static str> {

        match self {

            DoorState::Open => Ok(DoorState::Closed),

            _ => Err("Door is already closed or locked"),
```

```rust
        }
    }

    fn lock(&self) -> Result<DoorState, &'static str> {
        match self {
            DoorState::Closed => Ok(DoorState::Locked),
            _ => Err("Can only lock a closed door"),
        }
    }
}


fn main() {
    let door = DoorState::Closed;
    match door.open() {
        Ok(new_state) => println!("Door state: {:?}", new_state),
        Err(e) => println!("Error: {}", e),
    }
}
```

This implementation demonstrates how Rust's enums and match expressions enable clean and expressive code.

Embracing the Rust Ecosystem

Rust's ecosystem is an integral part of mastering the language. Tools like `Cargo`, `rustfmt`, and `clippy` streamline development, while libraries and frameworks expand Rust's capabilities. To maximize productivity:

- Use `cargo` commands for project management, such as `cargo test` for testing and `cargo bench` for benchmarking.
- Integrate `rustfmt` for consistent code formatting and `clippy` for linting and catching common mistakes.
- Explore popular crates on crates.io for reusable components.

For instance, automating code quality checks can be achieved with a `Cargo.toml` configuration:

```
[dev-dependencies]

clippy = "0.1"

rustfmt = "0.1"


[package.metadata.rustfmt]

edition = "2021"
```

Running `cargo clippy` and `cargo fmt` ensures your code adheres to best practices.

Looking Ahead

The future of Rust is bright, with a growing community and expanding ecosystem. Keeping pace with advancements is essential for staying relevant. Upcoming features like GATs (Generic Associated Types) and improved async support promise to make Rust even more powerful and expressive.

Engage with the latest developments by:

- Reviewing RFCs (Request for Comments) to understand proposed language changes.
- Participating in community discussions to shape the future of Rust.
- Experimenting with nightly builds to test bleeding-edge features.

Conclusion

Mastering Rust requires patience, practice, and a mindset of continuous learning. By embracing Rust's philosophy, building real-world projects, and engaging with the ecosystem, you will not only become proficient in the language but also contribute to its vibrant community. Rust is more than a tool—it is a way of thinking that empowers developers to build safe, performant, and future-ready software.

Chapter 12: Appendices

Glossary of Terms

This glossary provides definitions and explanations of key terms and concepts encountered throughout the book. Understanding these terms will help you navigate Rust programming with greater ease and clarity.

ABI (Application Binary Interface)

Defines how different program modules or components communicate at the binary level. Rust supports several foreign function interfaces (FFI) to interact with other languages like C.

Actix

A powerful and performant actor framework for building web applications and microservices in Rust. Known for its speed and scalability.

Borrowing

A core Rust feature that allows references to data without transferring ownership. Borrowing can be either mutable or immutable, enabling safe and controlled access to memory.

Cargo

The Rust package manager and build system. It simplifies project management by handling dependencies, building code, running tests, and more.

Crates

Rust's term for a package or library. Crates are the primary way to distribute and reuse Rust code. They can be published and shared on Crates.io.

Concurrency

The ability to run multiple tasks simultaneously, a feature that Rust handles efficiently using threads, async programming, and the ownership model.

Enums (Enumerations)

A Rust data type that allows the creation of custom data variants. Enums are used extensively for error handling and defining state machines.

FFI (Foreign Function Interface)

A mechanism that allows Rust to call functions written in other programming languages, like C or C++.

Generics

A feature in Rust that allows writing code that works with multiple data types. Generics make Rust programs more flexible and reusable.

Lifetime

A concept in Rust's memory model that determines how long a reference to data remains valid. Lifetimes are checked at compile time to ensure safety.

Macros

A powerful Rust feature for writing reusable and concise code. Rust macros differ from traditional macros in other languages as they work on the syntax level.

Match Statement

A control flow construct that allows pattern matching in Rust. It provides an expressive way to handle different possibilities in data.

Mutable

Refers to the ability to modify a variable or data structure. In Rust, mutability is explicit and must be declared with the `mut` keyword.

Ownership

The foundation of Rust's memory management system. Ownership defines how memory is allocated, accessed, and deallocated, ensuring safety without a garbage collector.

Pattern Matching

A feature used to destructure and match complex data types in Rust. It is often used with the `match` statement for clarity and control flow.

Rustacean

A colloquial term for a Rust programmer or enthusiast. The Rust community often uses this term to describe themselves.

Trait

A way of defining shared behavior in Rust. Traits are similar to interfaces in other programming languages but provide more flexibility and power.

Tuple

A compound data type in Rust that groups multiple values together. Tuples can hold different types and are commonly used for returning multiple values from functions.

Unsafe

A keyword in Rust that allows bypassing certain safety checks for performance or specific use cases. Unsafe code requires careful handling to avoid introducing bugs.

Vec

A dynamic array in Rust that allows storing multiple elements of the same type. It is part of Rust's standard library and widely used in collections.

Zero-cost Abstractions

A principle in Rust that ensures abstractions do not incur runtime performance penalties. Rust achieves this through its design and compile-time checks.

This glossary is intended to be a quick reference for important Rust concepts. Understanding these terms will solidify your grasp of the language and help you tackle complex Rust projects with confidence.

Resources for Further Learning

Rust is a vast and rapidly evolving language, with an active and supportive community. This section provides a comprehensive list of resources to help you deepen your understanding, stay updated, and explore specialized areas of interest. These resources cover official documentation, books, tutorials, online communities, and tools for mastering Rust.

Official Documentation

The Rust Programming Language (The Book)

The go-to resource for beginners and intermediate learners. Often referred to as "The Book," it provides a thorough introduction to Rust's core concepts and practical usage.

- **URL**: https://doc.rust-lang.org/book/

Rust Standard Library Documentation

A detailed reference for Rust's standard library, covering essential modules, traits, and functions.

- **URL**: https://doc.rust-lang.org/std/

Rust By Example

An interactive guide that teaches Rust through annotated examples. It's a great way to learn by doing.

- **URL**: https://doc.rust-lang.org/rust-by-example/

Rust API Guidelines

A comprehensive resource for creating idiomatic and ergonomic Rust libraries.

- **URL**: https://rust-lang.github.io/api-guidelines/

Books and Guides

Programming Rust (O'Reilly Media)

A deep dive into Rust's systems programming capabilities, including advanced topics like concurrency, unsafe code, and FFI.

- **Authors**: Jim Blandy, Jason Orendorff, Leonora F. S. Tindall

Rust for Rustaceans

Aimed at intermediate to advanced users, this book explores Rust's more complex features, such as lifetimes, ownership, and advanced traits.

- **Author**: Jon Gjengset

Practical System Programming with Rust

Focuses on real-world applications, including networking, embedded systems, and operating systems development.

- **Author**: Shing Lyu

Online Tutorials and Courses

Rustlings

An interactive set of exercises for learning Rust. It's perfect for beginners and covers topics like ownership, lifetimes, and traits.

- **URL**: https://github.com/rust-lang/rustlings

Exercism Rust Track

A platform offering coding exercises in Rust, with mentoring from experienced Rustaceans.

- **URL**: https://exercism.org/tracks/rust

The Rust Programming Language on Udemy

A popular course covering the fundamentals of Rust, including its unique memory management model.

- **URL**: Search for "Rust Programming" on Udemy.

Community and Forums

Rust Users Forum

A friendly and welcoming place to ask questions, share knowledge, and discuss Rust-related topics.

- **URL**: https://users.rust-lang.org/

Rust Discord

An active chat community for discussing Rust development, seeking help, and connecting with fellow programmers.

- **Invite Link**: https://discord.gg/rust-lang

Reddit

The r/rust subreddit is a hub for news, tutorials, and discussions about Rust.

- **URL**: https://www.reddit.com/r/rust/

Specialized Learning

Concurrency in Rust

Learn about asynchronous programming, thread safety, and concurrent data structures with these resources:

1. **Async Rust**: https://rust-lang.github.io/async-book/
2. **Rust Threads Documentation**: https://doc.rust-lang.org/std/thread/

Web Development with Rust

Explore Rust frameworks like Actix Web and Rocket for building web applications:

1. **Actix Web Documentation**: https://actix.rs/
2. **Rocket Framework**: https://rocket.rs/

Embedded Systems Programming

Dive into low-level programming for embedded devices using Rust:

- **The Embedded Rust Book**: https://docs.rust-embedded.org/book/

Game Development with Rust

Explore game development using Rust libraries and engines:

- **Amethyst Engine**: https://amethyst.rs/
- **Bevy Engine**: https://bevyengine.org/

Tools for Rust Development

IDEs and Editors

1. **Visual Studio Code**: With the Rust Analyzer extension for syntax highlighting, code completion, and debugging.
2. **IntelliJ Rust**: A comprehensive plugin for JetBrains IDEs.
3. **Neovim**: Enhanced with plugins like `rust-tools.nvim` and `coc-rust-analyzer`.

Debugging Tools

1. **GDB**: Compatible with Rust for traditional debugging.
2. **LLDB**: Often paired with the Rust-specific `rust-lldb`.

Profiling Tools

1. **perf**: A performance analysis tool.
2. **Flamegraph**: Visualize function call hierarchies and execution times.

```
// Example: Profiling with Flamegraph

fn main() {

    let numbers: Vec<i32> = (1..=1000000).collect();

    let sum: i32 = numbers.iter().sum();

    println!("The sum is {}", sum);

}
```

Keeping Up with Rust

1. **Rust Weekly Newsletter**: Stay updated with news, tutorials, and tools. Subscribe at https://this-week-in-rust.org/.
2. **Rust Conferences and Meetups**: Participate in events like RustConf and local Rust meetups.
3. **YouTube Channels**: Follow channels like "Jon Gjengset" and "The Primeagen" for Rust tutorials and live coding sessions.

Contributing to the Rust Community

Engaging with the Rust community is one of the best ways to learn and grow:

1. **Open Source Projects**: Contribute to projects on GitHub. Check out beginner-friendly issues with the `good first issue` label.
2. **Writing and Blogging**: Share your Rust experiences and insights by writing articles or tutorials.
3. **Rust RFCs**: Participate in shaping Rust's future by contributing to the Request for Comments (RFC) process.

By leveraging these resources, you can continuously enhance your Rust skills and become an active member of the Rust community. The journey of learning Rust is a marathon, not a sprint—so take your time and enjoy the process!

Sample Projects and Code Snippets

Exploring practical projects and dissecting code snippets is one of the most effective ways to understand Rust deeply. This section provides detailed examples, ranging from beginner-friendly exercises to more advanced applications. Each example highlights key Rust concepts, patterns, and best practices.

Project 1: A Command-Line Calculator

This project demonstrates the basics of handling user input, parsing strings, and implementing control flow.

Code Example

```rust
use std::io;


fn main() {
    println!("Welcome to the Rust CLI Calculator!");
    loop {
        println!("Enter an operation in the format: number1 operator
number2 (e.g., 3 + 2)");

        let mut input = String::new();

        io::stdin().read_line(&mut   input).expect("Failed   to   read
input");


        let              tokens:              Vec<&str>              =
input.trim().split_whitespace().collect();

        if tokens.len() != 3 {

            println!("Invalid input format. Try again.");

            continue;

        }


        let num1: f64 = match tokens[0].parse() {

            Ok(n) => n,

            Err(_) => {

                println!("Invalid number: {}", tokens[0]);

                continue;

            }

        };
```

```rust
    let num2: f64 = match tokens[2].parse() {

        Ok(n) => n,

        Err(_) => {

            println!("Invalid number: {}", tokens[2]);

            continue;

        }

    };


    match tokens[1] {

        "+" => println!("Result: {}", num1 + num2),

        "-" => println!("Result: {}", num1 - num2),

        "*" => println!("Result: {}", num1 * num2),

        "/" => {

            if num2 == 0.0 {

                println!("Error: Division by zero");

            } else {

                println!("Result: {}", num1 / num2);

            }

        }

        _ => println!("Invalid operator: {}", tokens[1]),

    }

    }

}
```

1. Handling user input with `io::stdin`.
2. Splitting and parsing strings.
3. Basic error handling with `match`.

Project 2: A Simple Web Server

This project uses the `tiny-http` crate to create a basic HTTP server. It introduces asynchronous programming and server-side development.

Code Example

```rust
use tiny_http::{Server, Response};


fn main() {

    let server = Server::http("0.0.0.0:8000").unwrap();

    println!("Server is running on http://0.0.0.0:8000");


    for request in server.incoming_requests() {

        println!("Received request: {:?}", request);

        let response = Response::from_string("Hello, Rust!");

        request.respond(response).unwrap();

    }

}
```

Key Concepts

1. Setting up a basic server using external crates.
2. Handling incoming HTTP requests.
3. Building a response and sending it back to the client.

Project 3: Fibonacci Sequence Generator

A classic problem that demonstrates recursion and efficient iterative solutions in Rust.

Recursive Approach

```rust
fn fibonacci_recursive(n: u32) -> u64 {

    if n <= 1 {

        return n as u64;

    }

    fibonacci_recursive(n - 1) + fibonacci_recursive(n - 2)

}
```

Iterative Approach

```rust
fn fibonacci_iterative(n: u32) -> u64 {

    let mut a = 0;

    let mut b = 1;

    for _ in 0..n {

        let temp = a;

        a = b;

        b += temp;

    }

    a
```

```
}
```

Key Concepts

1. Recursive function design.
2. Iterative optimization for performance.
3. Understanding Rust's u32 and u64 types for large numbers.

Project 4: File Operations

This project covers reading from and writing to files, a crucial skill for many real-world applications.

Code Example

```rust
use std::fs::{self, File};

use std::io::{self, Write, Read};


fn main() -> io::Result<()> {

    // Writing to a file

    let mut file = File::create("example.txt")?;

    file.write_all(b"Hello, Rust file operations!")?;

    println!("File written successfully.");


    // Reading from a file

    let mut file = File::open("example.txt")?;

    let mut content = String::new();

    file.read_to_string(&mut content)?;

    println!("File content: {}", content);
```

```rust
    // Deleting a file

    fs::remove_file("example.txt")?;

    println!("File deleted.");

    Ok(())

}
```

Key Concepts

1. File handling with `std::fs` and `std::io`.
2. Error handling with `Result` and the ? operator.
3. Basic file operations like create, read, and delete.

Project 5: Implementing a Custom Trait

Traits in Rust allow for defining shared behavior. This example implements a custom trait for a Shape struct.

Code Example

```rust
trait Area {

    fn area(&self) -> f64;

}


struct Circle {

    radius: f64,

}


struct Rectangle {
```

```rust
    width: f64,

    height: f64,

}


impl Area for Circle {

    fn area(&self) -> f64 {

        std::f64::consts::PI * self.radius * self.radius

    }

}


impl Area for Rectangle {

    fn area(&self) -> f64 {

        self.width * self.height

    }

}


fn main() {

    let circle = Circle { radius: 3.0 };

    let rectangle = Rectangle { width: 4.0, height: 5.0 };


    println!("Circle area: {}", circle.area());

    println!("Rectangle area: {}", rectangle.area());

}
```

Key Concepts

1. Defining and implementing custom traits.
2. Structs and method implementations.
3. Leveraging polymorphism through trait objects.

Best Practices in Rust Projects

1. **Use**   `Cargo`   **for**   **Project**   **Management**
   Always organize your projects using Cargo. It simplifies dependency management and builds automation.
2. **Write**   **Tests**
   Rust's testing framework is built-in and encourages robust testing. Use unit tests to validate functions and integration tests for modules.
3. **Adhere**   **to**   **Rust**   **API**   **Guidelines**
   Follow idiomatic patterns for designing public APIs, including naming conventions and modularization.
4. **Document**   **Your**   **Code**
   Use Rust's doc comments (`///`) to generate clear and concise documentation for your code.

```rust
/// Calculates the factorial of a number.
///
/// # Arguments
///
/// * `n` - The number to calculate the factorial of.
///
/// # Returns
///
/// The factorial of the number as a `u64`.
fn factorial(n: u64) -> u64 {
    (1..=n).product()
}
```

By exploring these sample projects and practicing with the provided code snippets, you'll gain hands-on experience with Rust's unique features and idiomatic practices. These foundational examples will prepare you for more complex and specialized Rust applications.

API Reference Guide

This section serves as a practical reference for commonly used Rust APIs. It provides detailed explanations and examples of core modules, traits, and functions from the Rust standard library. Each entry includes a description, usage examples, and notes on best practices to ensure optimal performance and clarity in your Rust projects.

---

1. `std::collections`

The `std::collections` module provides a wide array of data structures, such as vectors, hash maps, and binary heaps.

Example: Using a `HashMap`

```rust
use std::collections::HashMap;

fn main() {
    let mut scores = HashMap::new();

    // Insert key-value pairs
    scores.insert("Alice", 50);
    scores.insert("Bob", 60);

    // Access values
    if let Some(score) = scores.get("Alice") {
        println!("Alice's score: {}", score);
```

```
    }


    // Iterate over keys and values

    for (key, value) in &scores {

        println!("{}: {}", key, value);

    }


    // Remove an entry

    scores.remove("Bob");


    println!("Updated scores: {:?}", scores);

}
```

Key Notes

- **Best Use Cases**: HashMap is ideal for fast lookups and insertions.
- **Memory Considerations**: Ensure keys implement the Hash and Eq traits.
- **Common Alternatives**: Use BTreeMap for sorted keys.

---

2. `std::io`

The std::io module provides functionality for input and output operations, including reading from files and writing to the console.

Example: Reading a File Line by Line

```
use std::fs::File;

use std::io::{self, BufRead};
```

```rust
fn main() -> io::Result<()> {

    let file = File::open("example.txt")?;

    let reader = io::BufReader::new(file);


    for line in reader.lines() {

        println!("{}", line?);

    }


    Ok(())

}
```

Key Notes

- **Buffered Reading**: Use `BufReader` for efficient file reading.
- **Error Handling**: Handle `Result` and `Option` types carefully to avoid runtime errors.
- **Write Operations**: Use `write!` or `writeln!` macros for formatted output.

---

3. `std::thread`

The `std::thread` module allows for concurrent programming by spawning and managing threads.

Example: Spawning Threads

```rust
use std::thread;


fn main() {

    let handle = thread::spawn(|| {

        for i in 1..=5 {
```

```
            println!("Thread says: {}", i);

        }

    });


    for i in 1..=5 {

        println!("Main thread says: {}", i);

    }


    handle.join().unwrap(); // Wait for the spawned thread to finish

}
```

Key Notes

- **Thread Safety**: Use `Arc` and `Mutex` for safe shared state across threads.
- **Performance**: Avoid excessive thread spawning to prevent resource contention.
- **Alternatives**: Use async programming for lightweight concurrency.

---

4. `std::sync`

This module provides synchronization primitives like `Mutex`, `RwLock`, and `Arc` for shared state management in multithreaded programs.

Example: Shared State with `Mutex`

```
use std::sync::{Arc, Mutex};

use std::thread;


fn main() {

    let counter = Arc::new(Mutex::new(0));
```

```rust
    let mut handles = vec![];

    for _ in 0..10 {
        let counter = Arc::clone(&counter);
        let handle = thread::spawn(move || {
            let mut num = counter.lock().unwrap();
            *num += 1;
        });
        handles.push(handle);
    }

    for handle in handles {
        handle.join().unwrap();
    }

    println!("Final counter value: {}", *counter.lock().unwrap());
}
```

Key Notes

- **Arc**: Use `Arc` (Atomic Reference Counting) to share ownership safely.
- **Deadlocks**: Avoid nested locks to prevent deadlocks.
- **Alternatives**: Consider `RwLock` for read-heavy scenarios.

---

5. `std::time`

The `std::time` module provides tools for measuring time intervals and creating delays.

Example: Measuring Execution Time

```rust
use std::time::Instant;

fn main() {
    let start = Instant::now();

    // Simulate work
    for _ in 0..100000 {
        let _ = 42 * 42;
    }

    let duration = start.elapsed();
    println!("Time elapsed: {:?}", duration);
}
```

Key Notes

- **Performance Profiling**: Use `Instant` to measure precise durations.
- **Delays**: Use `std::thread::sleep` for implementing delays.
- **DateTime**: Use external crates like `chrono` for advanced date/time handling.

---

6. `std::env`

The `std::env` module allows access to environment variables and arguments passed to the program.

Example: Accessing Environment Variables

```
use std::env;


fn main() {

    if let Ok(path) = env::var("PATH") {

        println!("PATH: {}", path);

    } else {

        println!("PATH environment variable not found.");

    }

}
```

Key Notes

- **Cross-Platform**: Ensure environment variables are accessed in a platform-agnostic way.
- **Command-Line Arguments**: Use env::args for parsing arguments.

---

7. std::fs

The std::fs module simplifies file system operations, including creating, reading, and deleting files.

Example: Creating and Writing to a File

```
use std::fs::File;

use std::io::Write;


fn main() -> std::io::Result<()> {

    let mut file = File::create("output.txt")?;

    file.write_all(b"Hello, Rust!")?;
```

```
    println!("File created and written successfully.");

    Ok(())

}
```

Key Notes

- **Error Handling**: Always handle `Result` types returned by file operations.
- **Directory Management**: Use `std::fs::create_dir` and `std::fs::remove_dir`.

---

8. `std::option` and `std::result`

Rust's `Option` and `Result` types ensure safe handling of nullable and error-prone operations.

Example: Using `Result`

```
fn divide(a: i32, b: i32) -> Result<i32, String> {

    if b == 0 {

        Err(String::from("Division by zero"))

    } else {

        Ok(a / b)

    }

}
```

```
fn main() {

    match divide(10, 2) {

        Ok(result) => println!("Result: {}", result),

        Err(e) => println!("Error: {}", e),
```

```
    }
}
```

Key Notes

- **Chaining**: Use `?` to propagate errors.
- **Option Handling**: Use `unwrap_or`, `map`, and `and_then` for concise code.

This API reference guide covers a broad spectrum of Rust's standard library features. By leveraging these tools effectively, you can write robust, efficient, and idiomatic Rust code. Keep this guide handy as you tackle real-world projects and dive deeper into Rust's capabilities.

Frequently Asked Questions

This section answers some of the most common questions about Rust, covering topics from its core principles to advanced usage. These FAQs aim to clarify misconceptions, provide quick solutions, and deepen your understanding of the language.

---

1. Why does Rust have a steep learning curve?

Rust's learning curve is often described as steep because it introduces unique concepts, such as ownership, borrowing, and lifetimes, which are uncommon in other programming languages. These features are central to Rust's design and contribute to its memory safety and performance guarantees.

Tips to Overcome the Learning Curve:

Practice   Ownership   and   Borrowing
Write simple programs that focus on managing ownership explicitly. For example, practice moving   and   borrowing   values:
rust

```
fn main() {

    let s1 = String::from("Hello");

    let s2 = s1; // Ownership moved

    println!("{}", s2); // Works
```

```
    // println!("{}", s1); // Error: s1 no longer valid
}
```

1.
2. **Use**   **Rustlings**
   Interactive exercises like Rustlings can help reinforce these concepts.
3. **Start**   **Small**
   Focus on building small programs and progressively tackle more complex projects.

---

2. What is the difference between &T and &mut T?

In Rust, &T represents an immutable reference, while &mut T represents a mutable reference. The distinction is critical to ensuring safe access to data.

Example

```rust
fn main() {

    let mut value = 42;


    // Immutable reference

    let ref1 = &value;

    println!("Immutable reference: {}", ref1);


    // Mutable reference

    let ref2 = &mut value;

    *ref2 += 1;

    println!("Mutable reference: {}", ref2);

}
```

Key Points:

- Multiple immutable references are allowed simultaneously.
- Only one mutable reference is allowed at a time, and it cannot coexist with immutable references.

---

3. Why doesn't Rust have a garbage collector?

Rust uses a unique ownership model instead of a garbage collector (GC). Ownership enforces memory safety at compile time, eliminating the need for runtime garbage collection.

Advantages of No GC:

1. **Performance**: No GC pauses during execution.
2. **Predictability**: Memory is allocated and deallocated deterministically.
3. **Low Overhead**: Suitable for systems programming and embedded systems.

---

4. What are `lifetimes`, and why are they necessary?

Lifetimes in Rust specify the scope during which references remain valid. They prevent dangling references and ensure memory safety.

Example: Lifetime Annotations

```
fn longest<'a>(s1: &'a str, s2: &'a str) -> &'a str {

    if s1.len() > s2.len() {

        s1

    } else {

        s2

    }

}


fn main() {

    let str1 = String::from("Rust");

    let str2 = String::from("Ownership");
```

```
    let result = longest(&str1, &str2);

    println!("The longest string is {}", result);

}
```

Key Points:

- The 'a annotation links the lifetimes of input and output references.
- Lifetimes are often inferred by the compiler, reducing the need for explicit annotations.

---

5. How does Rust handle concurrency?

Rust's ownership model ensures safe and efficient concurrency. By design, data races are eliminated at compile time.

Common Concurrency Patterns:

1. **Threads**: Use std::thread to spawn threads.
2. **Async Programming**: Use async and await for lightweight tasks.
3. **Shared State**: Manage shared state with Arc and Mutex.

Example: Using async and await

```
use tokio::time::{sleep, Duration};


#[tokio::main]

async fn main() {

    let task1 = async {

        sleep(Duration::from_secs(1)).await;

        println!("Task 1 completed");

    };


    let task2 = async {
```

```
        sleep(Duration::from_secs(2)).await;

        println!("Task 2 completed");

    };


    tokio::join!(task1, task2);

}
```

Key Benefits:

- Rust avoids undefined behavior by enforcing compile-time guarantees.
- Concurrency tools are ergonomic and performant.

---

6. Why does Rust emphasize "zero-cost abstractions"?

Rust's zero-cost abstractions ensure that high-level constructs do not introduce runtime overhead. This principle applies to traits, generics, and iterators.

Example: Iterator Abstraction

```
fn main() {

    let numbers = vec![1, 2, 3, 4];

    let sum: i32 = numbers.iter().map(|x| x * 2).sum();

    println!("Sum of doubled numbers: {}", sum);

}
```

Key Points:

- Iterators compile to efficient, low-level loops.
- Rust prioritizes runtime performance without sacrificing code expressiveness.

---

7. How do I manage dependencies in Rust?

Rust uses `Cargo` to handle dependencies. Dependencies are specified in the `Cargo.toml` file.

Example: Adding Dependencies

```toml
[dependencies]

serde = "1.0"

tokio = { version = "1.0", features = ["full"] }
```

Key Commands:

- `cargo add <dependency>`: Adds a new dependency.
- `cargo update`: Updates dependencies to the latest compatible versions.
- `cargo doc --open`: Generates and opens documentation for dependencies.

---

8. How do I write tests in Rust?

Rust has a built-in testing framework. Tests are written using the `#[test]` attribute.

Example: Writing a Unit Test

```rust
fn add(a: i32, b: i32) -> i32 {

    a + b

}


#[cfg(test)]

mod tests {

    use super::*;
```

```
#[test]

fn test_add() {

    assert_eq!(add(2, 3), 5);

}

}
```

Best Practices:

- Use `assert_eq!` and `assert_ne!` for value comparisons.
- Organize tests in a `tests` module for clarity.

---

9. What is the difference between Box, Rc, and Arc?

These types provide different ways to manage heap-allocated data:

1. **Box**: Single ownership, used for dynamic sizing.
2. **Rc**: Reference counting for single-threaded programs.
3. **Arc**: Atomic reference counting for multi-threaded programs.

Example: Using Rc

```
use std::rc::Rc;


fn main() {

    let data = Rc::new(42);

    let rc1 = Rc::clone(&data);

    let rc2 = Rc::clone(&data);


    println!("rc1: {}, rc2: {}", rc1, rc2);

    println!("Reference count: {}", Rc::strong_count(&data));
```

}

---

10. How do I contribute to Rust?

Steps to Contribute:

1. **Learn the Rust Workflow**: Understand how Rust's RFC (Request for Comments) process works.
2. **Pick a Project**: Start with beginner-friendly issues tagged as `E-easy` or `good first issue`.
3. **Engage with the Community**: Join forums like the Rust Users Forum or Discord.

This FAQ section aims to address both fundamental and advanced Rust topics. By revisiting these questions regularly, you can solidify your knowledge and navigate Rust's ecosystem more confidently.

www.ingramcontent.com/pod-product-compliance
Lightning Source LLC
LaVergne TN
LVHW022341060326
832902LV00022B/4165